**The Internet of Money**

*Talks by Andreas M. Antonopoulos*

https://TheInternetOfMoney.org/

*Dedicated to the bitcoin community*

**Disclaimers:**

This book is edited commentary and opinion. Much of the content is based upon personal experience and anecdotal evidence. It is meant to promote thoughtful consideration of ideas, spur philosophical debate, and inspire further independent research. It is not investment advice; don't use it to make investment-related decisions. It's not legal advice; consult a lawyer in your jurisdiction with legal questions. It may contain errors and omissions, despite our best efforts. Andreas M. Antonopoulos, Merkle Bloom LLC, editors, copy editors, transcriptionists, and designers assume no responsibility for errors or omissions. Things change quickly in the bitcoin and blockchain industry; use this book as one reference, not your only reference.

References to trademarked or copyrighted works are for criticism and commentary only. Any trademarked terms are the property of their respective owners. References to individuals, companies, products, and services are included for illustration purposes only and should not be considered endorsements.

**Licensing:**

Almost all of Andreas's original work is distributed under creative commons licenses. Andreas has granted us CC-BY to modify and distribute the work included in this book in this way. If you would like to use portions of our book in your project, please send a request to licensing@merklebloom.com. We grant most license requests quickly and free of charge.

**Talks by Andreas M. Antonopoulos**

https://antonopoulos.com/

@aantonop

**Cover Design**

Kathrine Smith: http://kathrinevsmith.com/

**Transcription and Editing**

S.H. El Hariry, M.K. Lords, Pamela Morgan, Maria Scothorn, Sarah Zolt-Gilburne

**Copyediting**

Brooke Mallers, Ph.D.: @bitcoinmom

First print: **August 30, 2016**

Second print. **September 27, 2016**

Third print: **March 20th, 2017**

Fourth print: **October 1st, 2017**


Errata Submissions: errata@merklebloom.com

Licensing Requests: licensing@merklebloom.com

General: info@merklebloom.com

ISBN: 1537000454

# Table of Contents

## Praise for The Internet of Money

*I've always wondered what would have happened if we had built one-click payments into the browser from the very beginning. With bitcoin, we finally get this* Internet of Money. *But this book isn't just an ode to bitcoin — it's an ode to open protocols, what happens when you connect people online, and the power of innovation on the internet.*

— Marc Andreessen, co-founder Netscape and Andreessen Horowitz

*With Mastering Bitcoin, Andreas M. Antonopoulos wrote one of the best technical books on digital currency. With The Internet of Money, he's matched that feat by compiling his talks into one of the best books on Bitcoin for a broad audience. Highly recommended!*

— Balaji Srinavasan, CEO 21.co

*Over the past three years, awareness of the sweeping, transformative potential of bitcoin and its underlying blockchain technology has grown exponentially. That required people to grasp not only how this unorthodox technology worked but also its profound promise for society. No one has done more than Andreas Antonopoulos to get them over that hurdle. Read him. It will make you wiser.*

— Michael J. Casey, co-author *The Age of Cryptocurrency: How Bitcoin and Digital Money are Challenging the Global Economic Order*

# Preface

*By Andreas M. Antonopoulos*

When I started my journey in bitcoin, I never thought it would lead to this. This book is like an abridged diary of my discovery of bitcoin, delivered through a series of talks, starting in 2013 continuing to early 2016.

Over these past three years, I have delivered more than 150 talks to audiences across the world, recorded more than 200 podcast episodes, answered several hundred questions, participated in more than 150 interviews for radio, print and TV, appeared in eight documentaries and written a technical book called *Mastering Bitcoin*. Almost all of this work is available, for free, under open-source licenses, online. The talks included in this book are only a small sample of my work, selected by the editorial team to provide a glimpse into bitcoin, its uses, and its impact on the future.

Each of these talks was delivered to a live audience, without slides or any visual aides, and was mostly improvised. While I have a topic in mind before each talk, a lot of my inspiration comes from the energy and interaction with each audience. From talk to talk, the topics evolve as I try out new ideas, see the reaction and develop them further. Eventually, some ideas that start as a single sentence evolve, over several talks, into an entire topic.

This process of discovery is not perfect, of course. My talks are littered with minor factual errors. I recite dates, events, numbers, and technical details from memory and often get them wrong. In this book, my off-the-cuff errors, malapropisms, and verbal tics have been cleaned up by the editors. What remains is the essence of each presentation — how I wish it had been delivered, rather than a transcript of the actual delivery. But, with that cleanup there is also a price to pay. What is missing is the reaction and energy of the audience, the tone of my sentences, the spontaneous giggles from me and the people in the room. For all of that you have to watch the videos which are linked in Appendix A, *Video Links* of the book.

This book and my work over the past three years is about more than bitcoin. These talks reflect my worldview, my political ideas and my hopes, as well as my technical fascination and my unabashed geekiness. They summarize my enthusiasm about this technology and the astonishing future that I envision. This vision starts with bitcoin, a quirky cypherpunk experiment which unleashes a ripple of innovation, creating "The Internet of Money" and radically transforming society.

Almost the entire bitcoin community knows Andreas's contribution to bitcoin. In addition to his written and audio work, he's a highly sought-after public speaker, lauded for consistently delivering innovative, thought-provoking, engaging talks. This book represents only a small sampling of Andreas's work in the bitcoin and blockchain industry over the past three years. With so much content, simply deciding what talks to include was an arduous task. We selected these specific talks because they fit the criteria of the book; we could easily have included dozens more. This book is Volume 1; we hope to publish another volume soon.

We began this book project with a vision: to provide an easy-to-read, short-story style overview of why bitcoin matters, of why so many of us are excited about it. We wanted something we could share with family, friends, and co-workers that they might actually read: a compendium that they could pick up for five minutes, no-commitment, or explore for a few hours. It needed to be engaging, with real-world analogies to make the tech understandable. It needed to be inspirational, with a vision of how these things could positively impact humanity. It needed to be honest, acknowledging the shortcomings of our current systems and the technology itself.

Despite our best efforts, we're sure there are things we could improve and change; this is a first edition. We've edited heavily in some places, for readability, while always trying to preserve the essence of the talk. We believe we've struck a good balance and we're pleased with the book as a whole. We hope you are too. If you have comments about editing, content, or suggestions about how we can make the book better, please email us at errata@merklebloom.com.

**Tips to make your reading experience even better:**

**Each talk is intended to stand alone.** There is no need to start at the beginning — although if you are unfamiliar with bitcoin, you may want to start at the first talk, "What is Bitcoin," to get an overview of the topic. You'll notice some repeating themes and analogies, like the Red Flag Act or the parent-and-child talk about money. While the examples occasionally repeat, they're most often used to illustrate a different point in each talk.

**You'll find a robust index at the end of the book.** One of the things we're most proud of is the index. We've worked hard to provide an index that will allow you to cross-reference and research themes and topics.

# What Is Bitcoin?

*Disrupt, Start-up, Scale-up; Athens, Greece; November 2013*

Video Link: https://www.youtube.com/watch?v=LA9A1RyXv9s

*Reader note: This talk was given in late 2013. Bitcoin transactions are no longer free but fees are minimal. Currently, transaction fees are approximately 10 cents per transaction, regardless of the monetary value of the transaction.*

Good afternoon, Athens! Thank you for having me today. You want *disrupt*? I've got disrupt. I've got downright revolution. Today, we're going to talk about the most exciting, most interesting, and probably the most important technological invention in computer science of the last 20 years. I'm here to talk about bitcoin.

Bitcoin is digital money, but it's so much more than that. Saying bitcoin is digital money is like saying the internet is a fancy telephone. It's like saying that the internet is all about email. Money is just the first application. Bitcoin is a technology, it is a currency, and it is an international network of payments and exchange that is completely decentralized. It doesn't rely on banks. It doesn't rely on governments.

> *"Saying bitcoin is digital money is like saying the internet is a fancy telephone."*

We have never done this before in the history of humanity. This invention is truly revolutionary. When we look back, we will see that this is a historic moment in the evolution of computer science, but it is also a social and political revolution in the making. So, let's get started.

## Bitcoin, the Invention

Bitcoin is digital money. It is money just like euros or dollars, only it's not owned by a government. You can send it from any point in the world to any other point in the world instantaneously, securely, and for minimal or no fees at all. Two days ago, we saw one of the largest transactions ever recorded on the bitcoin network, where someone transferred $150 million between two bitcoin accounts, in one second, for zero fees. Just that allows you to grasp how disruptive this technology is going to be in terms of international payment systems. But this is just the beginning.

Bitcoin is a digital currency that came into existence in 2008 as an invention by a person called Satoshi Nakamoto. He published a paper where he posited that he had found the way to create a decentralized network that could achieve consensus, agreement, without any central controlling authority. Now, if you have studied computer science or distributed systems, this is known as the *Byzantine Generals' Problem*. It was first described in 1982. Until 2008, it was an unsolved problem. Then, Satoshi Nakamoto said, "I have solved it." Guess what happened next? Everybody laughed, ignored him, and dismissed him. He published his paper, and three months later, he published software that allowed people to start building the bitcoin network.

Bitcoin is not a company. It is not an organization. It is a standard or a protocol just like TCP/IP, or the internet. It's not owned by anyone. It operates by simple mathematical rules that everyone who participates in the network agrees on. Through this simple mechanism, through this invention of Satoshi Nakamoto, bitcoin is able to allow a completely decentralized network of computers to agree on what transactions have occurred on a network, essentially agreeing on who currently has the money.

So, if I send money from my account to somebody else's account in this peer-to-peer, completely decentralized network, it's just like sending an email. There's no one in the middle. Every ten minutes, the entire network agrees on what transactions have happened, without any centralized authority, by a simple election that occurs electronically.

This particular solution, this invention, is far more important than currency. Currency is just the first app—just the first application that you can build on a distributed consensus system. Other applications include distributed fair voting, stock ownership, asset registration, notarization, and many other applications we've never thought of before.

> *"This particular solution, this invention, is far more important than currency. Currency is just the first app."*

I discovered bitcoin for the first time in 2011, and since the internet, I have not felt so completely overwhelmed by the possibilities that I saw. I was there at the dawn of the internet in 1991 when it was pre-commercial. I could see that this was going to change the world but no one believed me. I have that exact same feeling about bitcoin.

Now, some of you may have heard of bitcoin, as a currency, is wildly high in price one day and wildly low in price the next. I'm here to tell you to ignore the price, to ignore bitcoin the money, and understand bitcoin the technology, the invention, and the network it creates. If we mess up the money, we'll just reboot another currency. The invention of bitcoin, the technology that makes it possible, cannot be uninvented. It creates the possibilities for decentralized organization on a scale never before seen on this planet.

*"The invention of bitcoin, the technology that makes it possible, cannot be uninvented. It creates the possibilities for decentralized organization on a scale never before seen on this planet."*

# Money of the People

Here's why bitcoin is important to me.

Approximately 1 billion people currently have access to banking, credit, and international finance capabilities—primarily the upper classes, the Western nations. Six and a half billion people on this planet have no connection to the world of money. They operate in cash-based societies with very little access to international resources. They don't need banks. Two billion of these people are already on the internet. With a simple application download, they can immediately become participants in an international economy, using an international currency that can be transmitted anywhere with no fees and no government controls. They can connect to a world of international finance that is completely peer-to-peer. Bitcoin is the money of the people. At its center are simple mathematical rules that everyone agrees on and no one controls. The possibility of connecting these 6 1/2 billion people to the rest of the world is truly revolutionary.

*"Bitcoin is the money of the people."*

Payment processors are going to be affected. These enormous companies charge higher fees to send money to poorer destination countries, a situation that is exploitative and corrupt. These organizations make enormous profits for a function that can be done in bitcoin nearly for free. As the adage of the entire internet once went, "I just replaced your entire industry with 100 lines of Python code," that's exactly what we're doing with bitcoin.

# Currencies, Businesses, and International Payments

How can you use bitcoin today? Simply speaking, bitcoin can operate as a currency. You can think of it as buying a foreign currency: You can connect to an exchange over the web, wire some euros, and use those euros to buy bitcoins at the current exchange rate. Yet, that's not really the best way to do it. We're entrepreneurs, right? We want to disrupt. The best way to do it is to find a product or service that you can offer that someone with bitcoin wants to buy, and start *earning* bitcoin.

## Solving Payment Problems

If you think about starting up a business in an international environment, there are two primary barriers to becoming a global business. The first barrier is that it is difficult to transport products and services across borders. With the internet, we solved that. We can now create products and services that are virtual, ones that we can sell anywhere in the world. So, we can deliver the product, but we still have one big problem: How do we get paid? Bitcoin solves that part. It allows us to receive payments from anywhere in the world, instantaneously. The bitcoin network allows any individual to send an amount that is as small as 100-millionth of a bitcoin, which in today's terms is a very tiny amount of money. You can't do that with today's money and payment systems. Credit cards were made in the 1950s, and they were most certainly not made for an internet age. Bitcoin is made for the internet age.

> *"Credit cards were made in the 1950s, and they were most certainly not made for an internet age. Bitcoin is made for the internet age."*

So, if you can suddenly send payments that are one-hundredth of a euro, or one-thousandth of a euro, you can sell content. You can do microtransactions. You can collect payments from millions of people in tiny amounts and make them, in aggregate, be worth something. On the same network where you can send one-thousandth of a euro or one-millionth of a euro, you can send a billion euros or a trillion euros. The fee will be exactly the same, because fees depend on the size of the transaction in kilobytes, not on the amount or content.

# Neutrality, Criminals, and Bitcoin

Let's look back at the internet and see what lessons we can learn about why bitcoin is important. One of the most important principles of the internet is neutrality. The internet does not distinguish between a large organization and a small organization. It does not know the difference between CNN and an Egyptian blogger. It allows the Egyptian blogger to speak to the world with the same power of voice that CNN has.

Bitcoin is neutral to the sender, the recipient, and the value of the transaction. That means it gives every citizen, every user of bitcoin, the ability to innovate in terms of financial instruments, payment systems, and banking. You can operate on the same level as Citibank. That is truly revolutionary.

*"Bitcoin is neutral to the sender, the recipient, and the value of the transaction. That means it gives every citizen, every user of bitcoin, the ability to innovate in terms of financial instruments, payment systems, and banking."*

It takes a hierarchical system of international finance and turns it on its head. Up to now, that hierarchical system has achieved security by limiting access, because that is the main method of trust in our payment systems—you can't get in unless you're vetted. Bitcoin creates a completely flat and decentralized network where every node is equal, where the protocol is neutral to the transactions, and it pushes innovations to the edge of the network, allowing exactly the same phenomenon we saw on the internet: innovation without permission. You don't need to ask anyone if your application can be published on the internet. You don't need to ask anyone to completely subvert a new industry with your information technology. On bitcoin, you don't need to ask anyone to invent a new financial instrument, a new payment system, a new service. You can just do it. You can just write the code, and you are now part of an international financial network that can run that code and put you in contact with millions of consumers.

*"On bitcoin, you don't need to ask anyone
to invent a new financial instrument, a new
payment system, a new service. You can just do
it."*

Now, it's still early days. We don't yet have the polished interfaces. It's difficult to use. It's used by criminals. It's used by various organizations around the world, and it's not easy to see exactly who is using bitcoin. I've heard all of that before. When I was on the internet back in 1991, it was a den of thieves, pornographers, pirates, and criminals. But it didn't matter then, and it doesn't matter now. It doesn't matter because the same powerful technology that can be used by a criminal to promote their criminal activities can also be used by all of the rest of us to do good, to do incredible things all across the world. And there are more of us than there are of them.

Bitcoin creates an environment that is ripe for innovation, because it's not just a currency; it's a technology, a network, *and* a currency. I can tell you today that I'm very happy that bitcoin's price is climbing very high, because I own some bitcoin and it feels kind of nice. But I don't care about the price. If bitcoin crashed tomorrow morning, the technology is still revolutionary. Just like if a website fails on the internet, or an application fails on the internet, the internet doesn't go away.

*"Bitcoin creates an environment that is ripe for
innovation, because it's not just a currency; it's
a technology, a network, and a currency."*

# Bitcoin as a Mechanism to Opt In and Opt Out

If you understand that bitcoin is a technology and not just a currency, you can truly grasp the importance it has. Again, it's not about us. It is about the other 6 1/2 billion. It is about the ability to bring to the world a level of financial integration that the world has never seen before. From our perspective in the privileged world, it is a great technology. We can do some disruptive innovation. We can build some interesting services. But if you're a Kenyan farmer who's trying to raise money in order to buy seed, and now you can do decentralized peer-to-peer lending and reach out to lenders from all across the globe, this is not just a technology—this is truly life-changing.

> *"Bitcoin is about the ability to bring to the world a level of financial integration that the world has never seen before."*

The vast majority of the world lives under repressive and corrupt regimes with central banks that impose hyper-inflation at 30 percent a month. It's much more important to see how bitcoin can affect all of those people. There are 2 billion people on the internet and only 1 billion of them have bank accounts. We can change that. It's not going to be easy, make no mistake about it. When you throw a disruptive technology in the middle of the most powerful organizations on the planet, they don't like it. Right now, we're still in the early stages. To use the trite expression, "First they ignore us, then they laugh at us, then they fight us, then we win." We're still at the laughing-at-us stage. That's quite all right, because by the time they get to fighting us, they've already lost. This technology just went global with the introduction of more than $2.5 billion from Chinese investors who discovered a counterbalance to the world domination of the global reserve currency of the US dollar.

## Altcoins: Currencies for Everyone

There are almost 200 currencies of the world, but there's only one international currency. There are almost 200 currencies controlled by central banks and governments, but there is only one mathematical currency today, and that is bitcoin.

> *"Cryptographic currencies are going to be a mainstay of our financial future. You cannot un-invent this technology. You cannot turn this omelette back into eggs."*

We are going to build more of them. Cryptographic currencies are going to be a mainstay of our financial future. They are going to be a part of the future of this planet because they have been invented. It's as simple as that. You cannot un-invent this technology. You cannot turn this omelette back into eggs. We already have over 100 competing currencies in the space, which shows how quickly innovation

7

has exploded, even beyond bitcoin the currency. There are many other alternative currencies — altcoins, as they're known—that use the same basic technology of a decentralized asset ledger using consensus in the network with Satoshi's algorithm. Some of these currencies are inflationary, some deflationary, some use demurrage or negative interest rates, some are charitable and redistribute a proportion of the income to charitable organizations.

We can invent money nonstop and create new forms of money and financial instruments.

*"At the end of the day, bitcoin is programmable money. When you have programmable money, the possibilities are truly endless."*

# Programmable Money for All of Us

At the end of the day, bitcoin is programmable money. When you have programmable money, the possibilities are truly endless. We can take many of the basic concepts of the current system that depend on legal contracts, and we can convert these into algorithmic contracts, into mathematical transactions that can be enforced on the bitcoin network. As I've said, there is no third party, there is no counterparty. If I choose to send value from one part of the network to another, it is peer-to-peer with no one in between. If I invent a new form of money, I can deploy it to the entire world and invite others to come and join me.

*"Bitcoin is the internet of money. Currency is only the first application. At its core, bitcoin is a revolutionary technology that will change the world forever."*

Bitcoin is not just money for the internet. Yes, it's perfect money for the internet. It's instant, it's safe, it's free. Yes, it is money for the internet, but it's so much more. Bitcoin is the internet of money. Currency is only the first application. If you grasp that, you can look beyond the price, you can look beyond the volatility, you can look beyond the fad. At its core, bitcoin is a revolutionary technology that will change the world forever.

Join me in the revolution.

Thank you.

# Peer-to-Peer Money

*Reinvent Money at Erasmus University; Rotterdam, Netherlands; September 2015*

Video Link: https://www.youtube.com/watch?v=n-EpKQ6xIJs

A lot of people ask me to talk about the latest things in bitcoin, but what I really want to talk about is ancient history. I want to provide a historical context for money and talk about why bitcoin is important in this historical context.

## How Old Is Money?

First, a little pop quiz for the audience: If you think of money as technology, as a technological system that human civilization has invented, how old is this technology? Any ideas? *Audience responds with wildly varying answers*

Lots of different answers here. It's always surprising to me that people say, it's 400 years old, 1000 years old, 2000 years old. In fact, we don't really know how old money is. Part of the reason we don't know how old money is, is because we have yet to discover a civilization so old that it didn't have money. We know money is as old as civilization.

> *"Money is as old as civilization."*

One thing that surprises people is that money is older than writing. We know this because when we look at archeological discoveries of writing, we find hieroglyphics and we find cuneiform. When we look at all of these ancient forms of writing, guess what they're writing about. Money. They're writing ledgers. All of the ancient writing we find, the first forms of writing, are ledgers. They are writing about money. Because money is older than writing.

Is money older than the wheel? I don't know, but we do know that wheels were used as money. Perhaps the first wheel was sold for money or was used as a form of money itself. Archeological sites going back into the Stone Age have revealed the presence of money in the form of shells and feathers and beads.

In fact, we can teach primates how to use money. There have been several studies where chimpanzees are taught how to use money. They are taught that a specific type of stone can be exchanged for bananas. Researchers then watch the monkeys to see what they will do with this new information. They very quickly invent armed robbery. They figure out that if you beat up the other monkey and take its stones, you can exchange them for bananas. Surprisingly, the second thing they invent is prostitution. They figure out that sexual favors can be exchanged for stones, which can be used for bananas. What does that tell you about the nature of money?

I think the important insight into the nature of money is that money is a form of communication. At its very basic level, money isn't value. Money represents an abstraction of value; it's a way of communicating value. It's a language. Therefore, money is as old as language because the ability to communicate value is as old as language and money. In many ways, it has characteristics that make it a linguistic construct. It's a form of communication.

> *"We use money to communicate value to each other, to express to each other how much we value a product, a service, a gesture."*

We use money to communicate value to each other, to express to each other how much we value a product, a service, a gesture. We use it as the basis of social interaction because by communicating value to each other, we create social bonds. So, money is also a very important social construct. This is an ancient technology. Yet, ironically, it's one of the technologies that is least studied from a historical and technological perspective. We look at bitcoin today and it represents an invention, a new form of money. Let's think about that for a moment.

# Technological Evolution of Money

How often has the technology of money been transformed by invention? How many different forms of money have existed? At a very basic level, a way to communicate value is to exchange things that we consider of equal value. "Here is a goat. I will take 20 bananas for my goat." That's not really money because it's a barter transaction, but it's the first form of communication about value.

## Barter to Precious Metals

Then, we start seeing abstract forms of money. The first major technological evolution is to start exchanging something that you can't eat—a feather, a bead, a string with knots on it, a colorful something that can be used for aesthetic purposes. That's when money takes an abstract form. The first major transformational technology moment for money was when money stopped being about the tangible consumption of intrinsic value, but became something that referred to value, as an abstraction.

> *"The first major transformational technology moment for money was when money stopped being about the tangible consumption of intrinsic value, but became something that referred to value, as an abstraction. One of the most popular forms of these abstractions was to use precious metals to express value."*

One of the most popular forms of these abstractions was to use precious metals to express value. Precious metals combine some of the most important characteristics of money: hard to find (scarce); easily transportable (at least when compared to a giant rock or a whole barrel of feathers); easy to divide (you can cut a gold coin into pieces and subdivide the pieces); and universally valued for aesthetic purposes. That's the second major transformation in money technology. It took hundreds of thousands of years before we saw the introduction of precious metals. Historically, we start seeing precious metals in the beginning of the agrarian civilizations in the Fertile Crescent area in the Middle East. The Babylonians, the Egyptians, and the Greeks developed these precious metals.

## Precious Metals to Paper

Two major technological evolutions and then nothing for a few thousand years. Then someone came up with a brilliant idea: If I deposit gold with someone trustworthy, they can give me a piece of paper that says that I have gold in this trustworthy vault. Then I could trade the paper instead of the gold. It's easier to carry. As long as I can trust that my money is in the vault, then I've got a new form of money.

With every technological evolution in money, there is skepticism. But I think this might be the moment of the greatest amount of skepticism in human civilization. For a lot of people, this new invention of money as paper was somewhat controversial. You think people are freaking out about bitcoin? Imagine how much they freaked out when you told them that now, instead of trading in gold, they would trade in pieces of paper. For a lot of people, this was unthinkable. I mean, after all, clearly this paper does not have any real value. It took about 400 years for paper, as money, to become accepted broadly. It was a big aberration.

*"You think people are freaking out about
bitcoin? Imagine how much they freaked out
when you told them that now, instead of trading
in gold, they would trade in pieces of paper."*

## Paper to Plastic

Then, about 60 years ago, we saw a new form of money in the form of plastic cards.
In fact, the first cards were paper again. In the United States, Diners Club was the
first to create a credit card, which was a form of traveler's cheque. Then, people
took that and they said, "This isn't money. Why don't you give me some of the
good old paper money that I know?" That was another big transformation in money.

## Plastic to Bitcoin

Now, we have bitcoin. Bitcoin is, in my mind, a pretty radical transformation. It's
as radical as the change from precious metals to paper money. Perhaps even more
radical. So what is bitcoin? The fundamental issue in describing bitcoin is that if
you use references to our existing experience, that experience is based on thousands
of years of understanding what money is in a very physical form. Now, we're trying
to explain a form of money that is completely abstract. "It's a token that represents
acceptance in a network, a network-centric form of money." But that doesn't even
begin to describe what this thing is.

One of the most common misunderstandings, when I try to describe bitcoin, is
that people think that it's simply a payment system, that bitcoin is simply a form
of digitization of money. It's digital money. Great. Well, that's kind of pointless
because we already have digital money. All of you use digital money every day,
long before bitcoin came along. You have bank accounts. Those bank accounts have
digital ledgers. You use those bank accounts to send payments electronically. That's
digital money.

*"Bitcoin is a fundamental transformation of the
technology of money."*

Bitcoin isn't just digital money. Bitcoin is a fundamental transformation of the technology of money. It's difficult to grasp because it's so different from everything we've known before. So, I will take a different stab at it. I want to take a look at network architecture for a second.

# Moving to a Network-Centric, Protocol-Based Era

Bitcoin is not happening in a vacuum. It's happening at a moment in history when we're seeing a transformation of many fundamental social institutions. That transformation is the great network-centric era.

For centuries, social institutions were organized around hierarchical organizations: institutions, democracy, banking, education. All of our social interactions were organized by appeal to authority in these hierarchies, these bureaucracies of people. But something happened with the invention of the internet. We started seeing more and more of these social institutions changing from systems that were closed, opaque, unaccountable hierarchical complexes with their own rules, into platforms. We started seeing the introduction of systems that have interfaces, API's that we can access, where information can flow in and out of the organization. So, we move from institutions to platforms.

Then, we start seeing an even more important transformation, when we move from platforms to protocols. The interesting thing about the change between a platform and a protocol is, when you have a protocol there is no central appeal. TCP/IP doesn't work in reference to a service provider. TCP/IP works without context everywhere in the world. You don't have to sign up for an account to use TCP/IP; you just have to use the language. Once you move from a platform to a language, it opens up all of these possibilities.

> *"Bitcoin is the first network-centric, protocol-based form of money. That means it exists without reference to an institutional or platform context."*

Bitcoin is the first network-centric, protocol-based form of money. That means it exists without reference to an institutional or platform context. I'll get back to that in a second, this is a really important point.

# Peer-to-Peer Architecture

We say that bitcoin is peer-to-peer money. What does that mean? It refers to an architecture used in terms of computer science or networking or distributed systems to describe the relationship between participants and a system. The architecture of bitcoin is peer-to-peer because every participant in the network speaks the bitcoin protocol on an equal level. There are no special bitcoin nodes; all nodes are the same.

Peer-to-peer means that when you send out a transaction to the network, every peer treats it the same. It has no context inside the peer's system other than what it gets from the network. An interesting issue in distributed systems is this issue of context and state. If you log in to Facebook and you have an account with Facebook, you're not using a protocol. All of the state is controlled by Facebook. You have a login session and all of the data is held by them. We call that architecture *client-server*. Bitcoin is different because it's peer-to-peer, just like email or TCP/IP.

# Client-Server Architecture

We are reluctant to discuss money. In fact, it's shocking that in almost all countries, money is not part of the education system. Five-year-olds have great questions about money. Most parents find it almost impossible to answer these questions. "What is money, Mommy? How does money work? Why do we not have more of it? Why can't everyone have more of it?" You don't say, "Suzy, go back to your room and study inflation, like a good girl, and don't come back until you understand the answer to those questions!"

We don't discuss money. It's interesting — we use a technology as a foundation of almost every aspect of social interaction, and yet it is a completely taboo subject. We all pretend that we don't particularly care about money, at least not intrinsically. We have higher goals and aspirations. We use it in everyday experience but we don't really talk about it. It's a dirty topic.

I think the architecture has something to do with it. Before bitcoin, the previous iteration of money — when money started being issued in exchange for precious metals stored in a vault — what that represented was a form of debt. That's a really important concept to understand because it colors our discussion.

*"Before bitcoin, the previous iteration of money — when money started being issued in exchange for precious metals stored in a vault — what that represented was a form of debt."*

How many of you have money in a bank? None of you has money in a bank. Do you store physical money in a safe deposit box? If so, maybe then you could say you have money in a bank. The rest of you have loaned your money to a bank. For the privilege of loaning your money to a bank, you will be paid the amazing interest rate of 0.00001 percent per year. Your bank will take that money, turn around, and loan it to the people standing next to you for 24.99 percent APR.

*"This is a client-server relationship. Because that money only exists as a form of debt in a ledger that you do not control. A ledger that is stored by a server, and you are simply a client. In fact, you have no control over it at all."*

This is a client-server relationship. Because that money only exists as a form of debt in a ledger that you do not control. A ledger that is stored by a server, and you are simply a client. In fact, you have no control over it at all. You don't even have basic interfaces to that money unless that interface is mediated by the server. That's what a client-server architecture does.

## Master-Slave Architecture

We have another term in distributed systems that describes a particular form of client-server architecture, where the secondary party only has a weak copy that isn't really meaningful. We call that a *master-slave architecture*. If you think of the previous iteration of money as a master-slave architecture, you have to ask an uncomfortable question: Who is the slave? Because in a system of debt, one of the two parties is always the slave.

*"...in a system of debt, one of the two parties is always the slave."*

You are the client. You are not the server. The server doesn't really serve you; they serve themselves because they're the master. That is the architecture of money we live in. That is the architecture of money we use in our civilization: an architecture of money where you have no control; an architecture of money where every interaction is mediated by a third party that has absolute control over that money.

Today, if you go to an ATM machine and you put in your card, the bank may decide to give you your money. One day—as the people of Cyprus, Greece, Venezuela, Argentina, Bolivia, Brazil, and a list of hundreds of countries over the last several decades and even centuries have discovered—one day, you go to the bank and the bank does not want to give you the money, because they don't have to. That's the essence of a master-slave relationship.

*"Bitcoin is fundamentally different because in bitcoin, you don't owe anyone anything and no one owes you anything. It's not a system based on debt."*

Bitcoin is fundamentally different because in bitcoin, you don't owe anyone anything and no one owes you anything. It's not a system based on debt. It's a system based on ownership of this abstract token. Absolute ownership. We have an expression in the United States, which is "possession is nine-tenths of the law." In bitcoin, possession is ten-tenths of the law. If you control the bitcoin keys, it's your bitcoin. If you don't control the bitcoin keys, it's not your bitcoin. You're back to a master-slave relationship.

*"In bitcoin, possession is ten-tenths of the law. If you control the bitcoin keys, it's your bitcoin. If you don't control the bitcoin keys, it's not your bitcoin."*

# Bitcoin, a Fundamental Transformation of Money

Bitcoin represents a fundamental transformation of money. An invention that changes the oldest technology we have in civilization. That changes it radically and disruptively by changing the fundamental architecture into one where every participant is equal. Where transaction has no state or context other than obeying the consensus rules of the network that no one controls. Where your money is yours. You control it absolutely through the application of digital signatures, and no one can censor it, no one can seize it, no one can freeze it. No one can tell you what to do or what not to do with your money.

It is a system of money that is simultaneously, absolutely transnational and borderless. We've never had a system of money like that. It's a system of money that transmits at the speed of light, one that anyone in the world can participate in with a device as simple as a text-messaging phone.

This represents a technological innovation that is terrifying to a lot of people because it is such a fundamental transformation of money. What they will tell you is that they're worried. They're very worried. They're worried that criminals will use bitcoin. But the truth is that they're far more terrified that all of the rest of us will.

Thank you.

# Privacy, Identity, Surveillance and Money

*Barcelona Bitcoin Meetup at FabLab; Barcelona, Spain; March 2016*

Video Link: https://www.youtube.com/watch?v=Vcvl5piGlYg

Today, I'm going to talk about the concepts of neutrality, decentralization, privacy, and what makes bitcoin so special. You've heard me talk a lot about bitcoin. When I use the word *bitcoin*, I am not talking about the currency. I am talking about a broader concept: the concept of completely decentralized, network-based, flat networks for providing trusted applications. If you happen to have a completely decentralized flat network that could provide trusted applications, the most logical first application is currency. But currency is just the first app.

## Banking: Liberator to Limiter

We are restructuring society by rebuilding institutions. Traditionally, our institutions have been hierarchical in design. This was an invention of industrialization, an 18th-century concept to allow people to organize and communicate at a larger scale. It was very effective at breaking the monopolies of kings and feudal systems. It has now run its course.

Sometimes people ask me what my political positions are, and it's very difficult to explain, but one word captures it, I think: I am a *disruptarian.* What that means is that every 30 or 40 years at least, things that have settled need to be disrupted. Because as they settle, power accumulates, they become centralized, and with centralized power, corruption happens. This isn't a new concept. My ancestors—I come from Greece—figured out that corruption happens in systems of power, and absolute power produces absolute corruption. There is no more absolute power than the power over money.

*"Every 30 or 40 years at least, things that have settled need to be disrupted. Because as they settle, power accumulates, they become centralized, and with centralized power, corruption happens. There is no more absolute power than the power over money."*

We live in a world where banking was once a great liberator. It was an invention that moved finance from the realm of kings to the realm of everyday people. That system liberated billions of people. And then it got concentrated, it acquired power, and the power led to corruption. What we're left with today is not a liberating system, and it's time to disrupt it. Bitcoin is one of the things that will greatly disrupt centralization of power. Why is that?

## Negative Outcomes by Design, Not Intent

One of the things that interests me as a computer scientist working in distributed systems is the architecture of systems. Architecture is a great topic for this city. The architecture of systems is what ultimately produces the outcomes.

I've worked with a lot of bankers. They're nice people. They try to feed their family, pay their mortgage, keep a steady job. Among them, there are a few sociopaths who inevitably rise to the highest positions of power because sociopathy is an advantage in hierarchical systems. But most of the problems with traditional concentration of power in money has nothing to do with the people being evil. It has to do with the fact that these institutions — through their shape, through their architecture — produce outcomes that are not good. They produce outcomes that are not egalitarian. They produce outcomes that are restrictive. They start to express nativism, nationalism, tribalism, class structure, and all of these things make the world a smaller place.

## Communications Expanding While Access to Banking Is Declining

In fact, over the last 15 years, we've seen the internet become an enormous power for the decentralization of communications. It has been a very liberating force. But if you look at economic inclusion and how banking works, we haven't expanded opportunity. We haven't expanded access. In fact, we're now regressing. Economic inclusion is decreasing.

The reason it's decreasing is because these isolated structures of finance, their very architecture, raise walls: national borders, class structures, and differences in how your money and your commerce are treated. We live in a world that is increasingly global and interconnected. There is even an emergent global culture through the internet. And yet our financial systems are parochial, insular, and they're separated.

> *"We live in a world that is increasingly global and interconnected, and yet our financial systems are parochial, insular, and separated."*

If you look at it from a network perspective, there are systems of money for transmitting small amounts and systems of money for transmitting large amounts. Systems of money for consumer payments, systems of money for business-to-business payments. All of these are separated geographically based on borders, legal jurisdictions, nation-states. What the structure produces is separation. It means that, as people, we are less and less free to transact with the rest of the world. Geopolitics is affecting finance in a serious way because the combination of state and money produces toxic results.

And we're about to disrupt all that.

# New Architecture, New Access

What bitcoin's architecture gives us is a new way of organizing the world, exactly the same way that the internet flattened access to communication and made every system that connects to it an equal peer. If I have an IP address, my packets are treated no differently than the packets of anybody else on the network. For the most part, that gives voice to everyone. It gives everyone the power of the printing press on a global scale. Bitcoin will do the same by giving everyone the power of banking on a global scale.

*"What bitcoin's architecture gives us is a new way of organizing the world, exactly the same way that the internet flattened access to communication and made every system that connects to it an equal peer."*

Think of it like desktop banking. In the way desktop printing, desktop publishing and websites changed communications, desktop banking — individually controlled banking with all of the power of the largest bank in the world — will create disruption.

Imagine a world where every person has the ability not only to execute transactions but also to create complex financial systems and instruments without asking for anyone's permission. Simply by connecting to the network, anyone can start a new application. Centralized systems can't do that.

In a centralized system, the further out you are, the less control you have. The closer you get to the system, and the farther you move up the hierarchy, the more controlled, the more limited the access is. But not with bitcoin. With systems like bitcoin, every node on the network has equal access to all of the financial services. In a centralized system, if you want to build a new application, you must first ask permission. And then permission is only granted if that application can apply to a very large population and be profitable.

On the internet or on bitcoin, all that is needed to start an application is two nodes, two people, two systems. They can start communicating, construct their own protocols, their own systems, and that application with only two people using it is just as valid as every other application on the network.

# Net Neutrality and Non-Discrimination

When you look at the internet, the fundamental misunderstanding is that people think that the power of the internet comes from the ability to transmit information fast. But the real power of the internet comes from net neutrality. Net neutrality is the concept that the internet does not discriminate based on source, destination or content.

*"Bitcoin is the first financial network that exhibits neutrality."*

Bitcoin is the first financial network that exhibits neutrality. In a bitcoin transaction, the network doesn't care about the source, the destination, the amount or what type of financial application it's supporting. The only relevant question is, did you pay a sufficient fee to use the network resources? And if you did, your application is valuable.

## There Are No Spam Transactions in Bitcoin

We have an interesting conversation happening in bitcoin right now. Perhaps some of you have heard the term "spam transactions." What is a spam transaction? What does it mean for a transaction to be "spam"? I think that term is meaningless because to decide which transactions are spam and which are not, you're making a top-down judgment. You're imposing, in the architecture, the choices of which applications are legitimate. Then the question is, legitimate to whom? The end user? There is no such thing as a spam transaction simply because if a transaction carries enough fee, that means that the sender of that transaction felt it was valuable enough to transmit—and therefore, it is a legitimate transaction. This replaces the concepts of control and content by making decisions about what is good, what is bad, what is legitimate, what is illegitimate, what is a valuable application, what is not a valuable application, with a simple market mechanism. If you paid essentially a tiny fee for your transaction, then because of the democratization of finance, your transaction is valuable and is not spam.

## Network-Centric Money

Starting in the 1970s, we have seen the world begin to adopt digital currencies. When people call bitcoin a "digital currency," they're missing the point. The euro is a digital currency, the US dollar is a digital currency. Less than 8 percent of these currencies exist in physical form; the rest is bits on ledgers. But the fundamental difference is that these ledgers are controlled by centralized organizations, whereas in bitcoin, they're not. Bitcoin has a decentralized network, an open network.

*"Bitcoin isn't a digital currency. It's a cryptocurrency. It's a network-centric money."*

Bitcoin isn't a digital currency. It's a cryptocurrency. It's a network-centric money. I really like the idea of a network-centric money. A network that allows you to replace trust in institutions, trust in hierarchies, with trust on the network. The network acting as a massively diffuse arbiter of truth, resolving any disagreements about transactions and security in a way where no one has control.

# Dreaming of Totalitarian Control over All Financial Transactions

Starting in the 1970s, our currencies began to be digital, but this is not the same "digital" as bitcoin. This started a dream for governments, the dream of being able one day to control every financial transaction of every human being on the planet in a way that everything was visible to the power structures. Where privacy dies. Where the ability to make a transaction immediately puts you under the lens of systems that surveil you. We have been creating a system of global financial surveillance, a system of totalitarian financial surveillance throughout the world.

*"This started a dream for governments, the dream of being able one day to control every financial transaction of every human being on the planet in a way that everything was visible to the power structures. Where privacy dies."*

That system, which requires identification and credit checking and limited access, is responsible for the fact that economic inclusion is regressing. It is responsible for the fact that 2 1/2 billion people have absolutely no access to banking. That's just the heads of household, not counting their families. That's not counting people who have limited access to banking in a single currency within a single border. If you count all of them, it's billions upon billions.

# Censorship of Financial Transactions

As a member of the privileged elite of the developed world, I have the ability to open a brokerage account in 24 hours, electronically. And within 24 hours, I can be trading in yen on the Tokyo stock market. I can be sending and receiving money anywhere in the world without really any limits. All I have to do is sacrifice my privacy and my freedom.

Because while I can do all of those things and they're very powerful, there are some things I can't do. I am not talking about buying drugs. That's not really that interesting. What I am talking about are simple things — for example, donating to an activist organization like WikiLeaks. A few years ago, WikiLeaks was completely cut off from the world's financial system simply with extrajudicial pressure applied on the few major payment providers: Visa, MasterCard, the banking transfer system, PayPal, etc. Without any legal process, without any conviction, and perhaps, in my opinion, without absolutely any crime other than revealing the truth of crime, WikiLeaks was cut off from the world's financial system. This is now happening not just to activist organizations; it's happening to entire countries.

The dream of nation-states, to create a totalitarian financial system, died on January 3rd, 2009, with the invention of bitcoin and the mining of the genesis block.

> *"The dream of nation-states, to create a totalitarian financial system, died on January 3rd, 2009, with the invention of bitcoin and the mining of the genesis block."*

# Network-Centric Money Is Censorship Resistant

Bitcoin is *censorship-resistant*. You may have heard this term. You cannot control where money is transmitted in bitcoin. It's not attached to identities or geography. In bitcoin, surveillance of everyone is not possible. In bitcoin, censorship resistance is an artifact that is created by neutrality, the architecture of a flat network without borders. The architecture of neutrality that doesn't ascribe any meaning to source, destination or value, is what creates censorship resistance.

# Sousveillance, Not Surveillance

Privacy is very important but it's a term that often has very deep political meaning. I like to juxtapose it to another term, *secrecy*. What is the difference between privacy and secrecy? Ultimately, and practically in today's vocabulary, privacy is the right of billions of individuals to not be surveilled. Secrecy is the power of the very few to escape accountability, to have no transparency.

We live in a world where every individual transaction you do through the financial system is cataloged, analyzed, and transmitted to intelligence services all around the world that collaborate, and yet we have no idea what our governments do with money. The financial systems of the powerful are completely opaque. Our transactions are completely visible through this system of surveillance. This world is upside down. Bitcoin rights it.

Privacy is a human right and secrecy is a privilege of power, and we need to be in a world where we have complete, ultimate, strong privacy for the billions of people. Because that is a human right, because that is a cornerstone of the freedoms of expression, association, political speech, and all of the other freedoms that are very much attached to privacy. We need to live in a world where secrecy is fickle and easily pierced, where power has to face accountability because they are under the spotlight of transparency. We need to flip the system upside down.

> *"Privacy is a human right. Secrecy is a privilege of power. We need to live in a world where secrecy is fickle and easily pierced, where power has to face accountability because they are under the spotlight of transparency."*

One of my favorite words is a French word: *sousveillance*. It is the opposite of surveillance. Surveillance means to look from above; sousveillance means to look from below. In their dream of nation-states controlling all of our financial futures, they made one major miscalculation. It's a hell of a lot harder for a few hundred thousand people to watch 7 1/2 billion. But what do you think happens when 7 1/2 billion of us stare back? When the panopticon turns around? When our financial systems, our communication systems, are private, and secrecy is an illusion that can't be sustained? When crimes committed in the names of states and powerful corporations are vulnerable to hackers and whistleblowers and leakers? When everything eventually comes out? We have a great advantage because the natural balance of the system is one in which individuals can have privacy but the powerful cannot have secrecy anymore. Bitcoin is one of the first steps in that.

> *"We have a great advantage because the natural balance of the system is one in which individuals can have privacy but the powerful cannot have secrecy anymore. Bitcoin is one of the first steps in that."*

# Banks for Everyone

The ability to transact across borders means that we will now be able to extend financial services to billions of people who have no access. Not through complicated technology necessarily. Sometimes I speak to various regional banks, the ones that are not afraid of bitcoin. They tell me things like 80 percent of our population is a hundred miles from the nearest bank branch and we can't serve them. In one case, they said a hundred miles by canoe. I'll let you guess which country that was. Yet, even in the remotest places on Earth, now there is a cell-phone tower. Even in the poorest places on Earth, we often see a little solar panel on a little hut that feeds a Nokia 1000 phone, the most produced device in the history of manufacturing, billions of them have shipped. We can turn every one of those into, not a bank account, but a bank.

> *"I don't have a Swiss bank account in my pocket. I have a Swiss bank."*

Two weeks ago, President Obama at South by Southwest did a presentation and he talked about our privacy. He said, "If we can't unlock the phones, that means that everyone has a Swiss bank account in their pocket." That is not entirely accurate. I don't have a Swiss bank account in my pocket. I have a Swiss bank, with the ability to generate 2 billion addresses off a single seed and use a different address for every transaction. That bank is completely encrypted, so even if you do unlock the phone, I still have access to my bank. That represents the cognitive dissonance between the powers of centralized secrecy and the power of privacy as a human right that we now have within our grasp. If you think this is going to be easy or that it's going to be without struggle, you're very mistaken.

# Bitcoin, the Zombie of Currencies

If you read anything about bitcoin, you'll see the very same things that they said about the internet in the early '90s. It is a haven for pedophiles, terrorists, drug dealers, and criminals. How many of you in this room have bitcoin? How many of you in this room are terrorists, pedophiles, drug dealers or criminals? *Audience laughs*

You see the thing about bitcoin is while they push this story, every now and then someone who has never heard of bitcoin notices an important thing: it's still not dead, which is always surprising because every two or three months there is an article that says it's dead. That's great marketing. Because every time someone hears it's dead and three months later they hear it's still not dead, they think, "Huh, this thing really tends to survive." I call bitcoin "the internet of money," but perhaps we should call it "the zombie of currencies." It is the currency that is the undead.

> *"I call bitcoin the internet of money, but perhaps we should call it the zombie of currencies. It is the currency that is the undead."*

The issue here is that we're now creating a system that is threatening the largest industry in the world, and that is finance. They are going to object. They are going to push back, and they're going to use the most common and effective emotional tactic there is, which is fear. They will treat you in such a way as if you are idiots and try to persuade you that this is something to fear. When people hear that message, maybe the next day they come to one of these meetups and they meet a dentist who owns bitcoin, an architect who owns bitcoin, a taxi driver who uses bitcoin to send money back to their family—normal people who use bitcoin to give themselves financial power and financial freedom. Every time that message is broken by cognitive dissonance, bitcoin wins. All bitcoin really has to do is survive. So far, it's doing pretty well.

# Currencies Evolve

In the new network-centric world, currencies occupy evolutionary niches. They evolve, like species, based on the stimulus they have from their environment. Bitcoin is a dynamic system with software developers that can change it. The question is, in which direction will bitcoin evolve? Which environmental niche will it attempt to fit in? And how will that be affected by the actions of the powerful? If they attack bitcoin, it evolves to defend itself against predators, just like any species. If they attack bitcoin anonymity, it evolves to become more anonymous. If they attack its resilience, it evolves to become more decentralized. In the end, despite all of the messages of fear, bitcoin is the cuddly little bear of currencies and you do not want to kick it. Because, as in evolution, if you stomp on the little gecko, it will evolve until it's a Komodo dragon and then you can't stomp on it.

Sometimes people ask me, "Do you think governments will ban bitcoin? Do you think they will try to regulate it out of existence? Do you think they will attack it with denial-of-service attacks?" The answer is really simple because in network-centric systems—systems that are dynamic and adaptable, systems that exhibit antifragility — attacks cause the system to adapt and evolve and become resistant. Think about this for just a second.

*"In network-centric systems, attacks cause the system to adapt, evolve, and become more resistant."*

## Attacks Build Resistance

I've been involved with the internet since 1989. In the early days lots of articles were written about how the internet was not resilient, could not scale to do voice, was not secure. I remember times when denial-of-service attacks would take down Yahoo, AltaVista, and even Google for hours, sometimes days. What happened between then and now? How many times have you seen Google go down in the last five years? Have people stopped attacking Google? Quite the opposite. Google can now sustain gigabits of denial-of-service anywhere in the world and dynamically reroute. The same applies for all internet applications. The attacks didn't stop. The system became immune because, like a human immune system, if you are exposed to a virus and it doesn't kill you, you evolve resistance, and the next time you're exposed to the virus, it does nothing to you.

Will governments try to ban bitcoin? Regulate bitcoin? Attack bitcoin? They already are. They have been, almost since the beginning, and bitcoin is still getting stronger. It's a system that is under a constant denial-of-service attack, that is on the internet being attacked by hackers, by agents, by other systems, 24 hours a day.

*"Bitcoin is still getting stronger. It's a system
that is under a constant denial-of-service attack,
that is on the internet being attacked by hackers,
by agents, by other systems, 24 hours a day."*

In security, we have a really funny term, which is a *honeypot*. A honeypot is a system that is designed to attract hackers. What bigger honeypot could you have than a financial network that has $6 billion on it? If you hack bitcoin, there is a $6 billion reward for you finding a way to hack it. No one has collected that reward yet, and it's not because they haven't been trying. They've been trying nonstop. But systems like bitcoin are resilient.

# Welcome to the Future of Money

Remember that what we're doing here is not a currency. It is a reworking of the societal systems of organization that have failed us. The 18th-century systems of hierarchies that do not scale to a global, interconnected world are being replaced by network-centric, flat architectures—whether that's the internet or any of the applications running on top of it or bitcoin itself. Currency is just the first app. When you have a network that can provide you with neutral trust, you can build myriads of applications on top, and you don't have to ask for permission.

Bitcoin is much more than currency. When I say that bitcoin is "the internet of money," the emphasis is not on "money"; the emphasis is on *internet*. Welcome to the future of money.

Thank you.

# Innovators, Disruptors, Misfits, and Bitcoin

*Maker Faire; Henry Ford Museum, Detroit Michigan; July 2014*

Video Link: https://www.youtube.com/watch?v=LeclUjKm408

*Just before this presentation began, attendees viewed a video presented by the museum about the history of the automobile. That is the video referenced throughout this talk.*

Good morning. Now that was a fun video, wasn't it? About a month ago, I sold my car for bitcoin. That was an interesting experience, a whole new world. How many here have bitcoin? Of those who don't, how many of you have heard of bitcoin? *95% of audience has heard of bitcoin.* Anybody who has not heard of bitcoin? Okay, great, this is going to be a lot easier than I thought.

## Recognizing Innovation

Bitcoin is the internet of money, but it's a lot more than that. For this audience in particular and for the people who are here at the Maker Faire, I want to talk about bitcoin from the perspective of the misfits, the weirdos, the freaks. The people who refuse to think the way everybody else thinks. The people who see a half-working, elegant technology and don't look at the *half-working*; they look at the *elegant* side. They recognize innovation. And they recognize innovation, not just a few months or a few years before others, but sometimes a decade before others. Those are the kinds of people that come to Maker Faire. And so it's a great place to start talking about bitcoin.

Bitcoin is unexpected. Bitcoin is not money as we know it. Bitcoin should not have happened. Bitcoin really has no possibility of success. It can't possibly work. It's one of those things that does not work in theory, but it works in practice. Like Wikipedia. Like Linux. Like the internet. Weird ideas made by people with ponytails and neckbeards. Weirdos nobody really trusts.

Bitcoin succeeds because it works. As a technology, it's elegant. I want to talk about that spirit of the misfit. About walking into an industry boardroom saying, "You know what? We're about to change everything," and being laughed out of the room. Then, keeping on and going on, until, in fact, they change everything. This happens in technology all the time. We just forget about it. We ignore it. We rewrite the history in glowing terms.

# The Dangers of Automobiles, Electricity, and Bitcoin

We just watched a video about the early automobile. Do you know what the media said about the early automobile? They ridiculed cars. They mocked cars. Cars were slower than horses. Cars broke down all the time. Cars needed expensive gasoline that you couldn't find anywhere. They required enormous amounts of infrastructure to work. The media focused on the part of the story that sold the most papers: car accidents, pedestrians mangled by cars. For more than two decades from the first cars, the story was that of infernal, disgusting, dirty, noisy machines that were far inferior to horses, that couldn't go anywhere, that only weirdos would use, and that, most of the time, killed the occupants and everyone who came anywhere near them.

> *"For more than two decades from the first cars, the story was that of infernal, disgusting, dirty, noisy machines that were far inferior to horses, that couldn't go anywhere, that only weirdos would use, and that, most of the time, killed the occupants and everyone who came anywhere near them."*

This hysteria got so bad that in 1865 in the UK, they passed a law called the Red Flag Act. The Red Flag Act required that any operator of a vehicle have three crew members on staff: a driver, an engineer, and a flagman. The driver would operate the vehicle, the engineer would supervise that operation (think railroads), and the flagman would carry a red flag and run 100 yards ahead of the car to warn pedestrians of the imminent arrival of an infernal death machine that was going to mow them down.

Guess what happened to the UK? They lost the automobile-industry race because they saw that technology and, instead of seeing potential, they allowed fear to define their reaction. They created an environment where a car could not do the things that a car can do. If you make a car go as slow as the pedestrian who's running ahead of it with a red flag, you lose all of the advantages of a car. If a car requires a three-person crew to operate, you lose the advantages of a car. They tried to take the car and understand it from the perspective of railroads and horses. They failed. They lost the race.

What you didn't see in this video is that until that time, they were winning. The first really practical cars were built in England. They had already won the race in the Industrial Revolution with the steam engine. At that time, England was a powerhouse of industrial innovation. They were winning, until they decided that this dirty machine should be confined to a very limited space and set of rules. They killed the goose. No more golden eggs for them.

> *"The first really practical cars were built in England... At that time, England was a powerhouse of industrial innovation. They were winning, until they decided that this dirty machine should be confined to a very limited space and set of rules."*

That is instructive because this happens again and again in technology. When electricity was first domesticated and people started electrifying their homes, do you think the media announced, "This is brilliant! Edison's a genius! This is going to change the world!"? No. What they said was that this was dangerous technology that would burn down people's homes. They ran story after story after story about people getting electrocuted, about homes burning down.

> *"When electricity was first domesticated and people started electrifying their homes, do you think the media announced, This is brilliant! Edison's a genius! This is going to change the world!? No. What they said was that this was dangerous technology that would burn down people's homes."*

Of course, you couldn't really use electricity because it required a complete overhaul of your house. You had to put wires in your house, the wires that would burn it down. You'd have to buy special devices to connect to these wires, just before your house burned down. Only the rich could afford it. Clearly, this was a technology that was just an affectation of the rich. It was just a plaything with no practical value.

The mayor of Paris, during the World's Fair of 1900, said, "After the fair is over, this fad of electricity will be forgotten as quickly as the lights turn off." Famous last words are very common in technology, words that in retrospect look ridiculous. Like the head of IBM who once said, "I foresee a need for no more than five computers worldwide." Like the people who said that the telephone would never succeed.

> *"Famous last words are very common in technology, words that in retrospect look ridiculous."*

Can you guess what people are saying about bitcoin? They're telling you that it is a technology that is weird and complicated. A technology that caters to misfits, drug dealers, degenerates, pornographers, terrorists, thieves, swindlers. I don't see any of those people in this room but we better be careful just in case they show up.

Of course, they're wrong. Bitcoin is none of those things. Bitcoin is simply a technology. As a technology, often the first use it finds is in the hands of criminals. The first cars were used as getaway vehicles. The first telephones were used to plot conspiracy. The first telegrams were used to run long-distance mail-fraud schemes and Ponzi schemes. The first forms of electricity were used to run medical hoaxes and scam people. These things always happen with a new technology, and they happen with bitcoin, too.

> *"Bitcoin is simply a technology. As a technology, often the first use it finds is in the hands of criminals. The first cars were used as getaway vehicles… Criminals use the most cutting-edge technology because they operate in an environment with very high profit margins and very high risk."*

Why do you think criminals use technology like that? We could be moralistic about it and look at the actual reasons. Criminals use the most cutting-edge technology because they operate in an environment with very high profit margins and very high risk. In that environment, competition is fierce. Using the latest technology if you're already taking enormous risks isn't that big of a deal. And if you win, it gives you an enormous advantage. Throughout history, the most amazing technology is adopted by criminals first. I don't think that's necessarily what we want to put on the bitcoin marketing plan, but it's interesting to look at what criminals do and how that ends up being mainstream technology a decade later. There's a certain dynamic there.

Bitcoin is already way past its early stage and is no longer the purview of criminals. In fact, arguably it really wasn't in the first place, despite what the media said. Now, bitcoin is hitting the mainstream and things are changing very rapidly.

*"With bitcoin as a technology, something very exciting is happening. Something is going to shake up our financial and banking system as much as cars shook up the horse industry, as much as oil shook up the whaling industry, as much as electricity shook up the wood stove industry."*

Today I'm going to talk about bitcoin as a technology because something very exciting is happening. Something is going to shake up our financial and banking system as much as cars shook up the horse industry, as much as oil shook up the whaling industry, as much as electricity shook up the wood stove industry. Banking is about to be disrupted. Arguably, it's already being disrupted. In fact, by the time they figure out how serious this destruction already is, the game's already over. That's usually the case.

## Incumbent Reactions to Innovation

When established, entrenched industries first see a new disruptive technology, they ignore it because it can't possibly pose a threat. From the benefit of incumbency, from the high perch of an established monopolistic business, these threats look like children playing around. To JPMorgan Chase, bitcoin is like a lemonade stand trying to take on Walmart. If the technology continues to exist, then they go into the next phase where they start mocking the technology. They suddenly see it everywhere and they start making jokes about it. So, just like with the automobile, the first people who bought cars were mocked. They were shown always on their knees with a spanner, trying to fix their machine that had broken down again. That was the image of an automobile owner for the first years.

While they mock it, bitcoin continues to grow and improve. After a while, you see a change. At first, some of the incumbents in the industry say, "Hey, maybe we need to experiment with this. Maybe we need to start looking at this." Then there's a stampede because suddenly they realize *this is going to change our industry forever*.

By that time, it's too late. By that time, they're Kodak: going from number one in the world to, within three years, losing a $12 billion industry right out from under their feet to a company they had never even heard of before. A company that didn't even make cameras. Do you know who destroyed Kodak? A little Finnish company they had never heard of called Nokia. A company that didn't make cameras—until they did. Within three years they made half a billion cameras and destroyed Kodak. Tower Records dominated the music industry. Within four years they disappeared. Why? Because MP3s gave people choice.

IBM used to be the most unshakable company in computers. They guaranteed quality. In fact, buying anything but IBM was a sure sign that you were a loser. Then Linux happened. Linux shook IBM to the core because it subverted the very basic idea that in order to deliver quality engineering, in order to deliver the best computers possible for the serious work of banking, engineering, and government operations, you needed IBM. You needed a closed, controlled, carefully organized system built by serious Ph.D. engineers.

Back in 1992 when Linus Torvalds said, "I'm going to build an operating system in my dorm room because I can't afford to buy an operating system," that idea seemed completely preposterous. Operating systems were enormous edifices of complexity that took thousands of engineers to build. Linus Torvalds started simple; he started building an operating system. Six years later, Linux had started dominating the computing industry and Sun Microsystems was beginning to feel the pain. Eight years later, Sun Microsystems was heading into bankruptcy, HP was getting bought, their computer division was shutting down, and IBM stepped out of the personal-computing business.

Now, 80 percent of the cell phones on the planet run Android — which, by the way, is Linux. The servers they connect to run Linux. The banks we use run Linux. The entertainment systems we use run Linux. The cars we drive run Linux. You can always tell if they stop running Linux: the little blue screen that greets you that says, *Bleh. Sorry. Crashed. Wrong choice of operating system*. You get into a plane, the entertainment system boots up, it's running Linux. If you said to an IBM engineer 15 years ago, "You are about to be destroyed by an operating system built by a Finnish student in their dorm," they would have laughed at you.

*"If you said to an IBM engineer 15 years ago,*
*You are about to be destroyed by an operating*
*system built by a Finnish student in their dorm,*
*they would have laughed at you."*

Here we are today, and bitcoin is taking on the entire banking system, the most powerful industry in the world. Guess what? Bitcoin's going to win. It's going to win for a very simple reason. It's not just going to win because it's better. It's not just going to win because the banking system is run by gangsters, crooks, and some of the most immoral empty suits in the world. It's not just going to win because the banking system has spent the last 50 years delivering just two consumer innovations — ATMs and credit cards — and then spent the rest of the time trying to figure out how to fleece you. It's going to win because it's open. In a world of tinkers, of experimenters, of makers, open wins. The reason it wins is that it allows innovation to flourish at the edges.

*"Bitcoin is going to win because it's open. In a*
*world of tinkers, of experimenters, of makers,*
*open wins. The reason it wins is that it allows*
*innovation to flourish at the edges."*

# Open Innovation and Opt-In Systems

Let me explain what I mean by that. Every single financial system in the world has a security and trust model that requires excluding bad actors. I can't connect to the Visa network and program it because doing so would endanger the security of the Visa network. I can't connect to the SWIFT network, the worldwide interbank wire transfer network, because doing so would endanger the security of that network. All of these networks are designed to be closed because their primary security relies on access control. Very carefully vetting every single person who has access and touches the code. Very carefully vetting all of the applications that run on that system, because if they allow one bad actor into the heart of the system, that security is gone. That one bad actor can take over and do whatever they want. Of course, in 2008 we discovered that the bad actors owned the banks. And they did take over. They destroyed millions of homeowners, millions of retirees, and millions of savers all around the world with their greed.

> *"Bitcoin is different because it doesn't depend on access control to remain secure. It depends on a simple mathematical formula of incentives and rewards."*

Bitcoin is different. The reason it's different is not because we've suddenly found the most honest people in the world. Or because there are no quirks in bitcoin. Or because the network doesn't get attacked. Bitcoin is different because there are plenty of crooks in bitcoin — the network gets attacked all the time — but it doesn't depend on access control to remain secure. It depends on a simple mathematical formula of incentives and rewards. In order to participate in the bitcoin network and secure the network as a miner, which is a special function in bitcoin, you have to use a lot of computing power and spend a lot of electricity. If you win that competition, you get bitcoin as a reward. That simple equation creates a system of incentives where it's far better to play *with* the rules than against the rules. It's game theory. It's like a giant game of Sudoku.

If you look at that as a computer scientist, or even more as a banker, you say, "That can't possibly work. What do you mean it's a giant game of Sudoku and everybody is competing against each other? That's not the basis of a security system. That would bring chaos." It's kind of like "What do you mean it's an encyclopedia that anyone can edit? That would bring chaos" — said the Encyclopedia Britannica. If you're under 40, you've never heard of it.

Bitcoin is a completely open network. Anyone can connect to it. You can write an application right now, connect to the bitcoin network, and teach it to do something new. You can write a new financial service. You can write a new financial instrument. When you do so, you don't have to identify yourself to the network, you don't have to get permission from anyone. You don't have to be vetted. You don't have to be secured. The network doesn't fear you because its security doesn't depend on keeping bad actors out. In fact, bitcoin works fine with plenty of bad actors right in the core of the system because there is no core of the system; there is no center. It's a completely decentralized system. What happens when you create a network where open access to financial services is possible? Where, for the first time in history, anyone can connect and write an application?

*"Bitcoin is the internet of money, and currency is just the first application."*

Bitcoin isn't currency. That's a really important thing to realize. Currency is an app that runs on the bitcoin network. Bitcoin is the internet of money, and currency is just the first application. Today, there are a thousand companies writing the next app. Those companies are hiring tens of thousands of people in one of the most vibrant industries we have seen in the last two decades. In 2014, bitcoin startups will receive more than $250 million of investment. What's remarkable about that is that it's faster than the rate of investment in the internet in 1995. We are ahead of the curve. Bitcoin is growing faster than Twitter did in the first three years. Bitcoin is growing faster than Facebook grew in the first few years. The reason for that is because every misfit, weirdo, freak, or programmer from anywhere in the world can now connect to bitcoin without asking anyone's permission and take their weirdo misfit idea and build a new financial service. A new banking application. A new shopping application. A new escrow application. And that's exactly what people are doing. They are building things that are innovative, new, and brilliant. Things that we've never seen in banking before. Things that wouldn't get past the first planning meeting in your average bank because they'd get shot down.

*"When you have these two environments running side by side — the banking environment where everything requires permission, which is most certainly not granted, and a system which is completely open, where innovation happens on the edge without permission — guess who wins. Guess where all of the exciting things happen."*

When you have these two environments running side by side — the banking environment where everything requires permission, which is most certainly not granted, and a system which is completely open, where innovation happens at the edge without permission — guess who wins. Guess where all of the exciting things happen. Guess where all of the innovation happens. This is innovation that serves consumers.

*"Bitcoin is an opt-in system. You choose to use it. You choose what apps you're going to run. You choose who you're going to interact with. You choose the rules of the game by which you're going to interact. That's why bitcoin is going to win. It delivers innovation that consumers want and need."*

No one is sitting on bitcoin and trying to find a way to front run a high-frequency trading algorithm so they can squeeze 3 microcents about four microseconds faster than the other giant bank that's playing with algorithms. No one's trying to find a way to screw you out of your overdraft facility, an innovation that was pioneered by one of the big banks, I think in 2007. They realized that if you were close to the overdraft limit, if instead of running the big transaction first they flipped the order of the transactions and ran a lot of small ones, you'd pay a 25-dollar fee for every one of them, and they could maximize their fees. That's the kind of innovation they were focused on. So, they innovated more ways to screw their customers.

In bitcoin, nobody's doing that kind of innovation. The reason they're not doing that kind of innovation is because in bitcoin you can't force someone to take your app. If you bank with a big bank, it's *their* network, it's their policy, you're using their debit card, playing by their rules, and if you don't like it, you can go elsewhere and discover that they're all the same. Bitcoin is an opt-in system. You choose to use it. You choose what apps you're going to run. You choose who you're going to interact with. You choose the rules of the game by which you're going to interact. If you don't like an app, you don't download it. If you love an app, you download it and you tell all your friends about it. That's why bitcoin is going to win. It delivers innovation that consumers want and need.

# Including 6.5 Billion People in a Global Economy

There's another reason bitcoin will win. There is a massive imbalance that most people here don't notice. Every person in this room has access to a bank account without currency controls. A bank account from which they can buy and sell any currency in the world. A bank account from which they can wire money anywhere in the world. A bank account from which they can access international markets like the Tokyo Stock Exchange or the German stock exchange. A market from which they can access credit and liquidity. Auto loans and mortgages. A bank account which is powerful. That power is available to about a billion people on this planet. A billion people who have access to full-fledged, international, high-liquidity banking facilities.

There are 2 billion people who have no bank accounts at all. There are another 4 billion people who have very limited access to banking. Banking without international currencies, banking without international markets, banking without liquidity. Bitcoin isn't about the 1 billion. Bitcoin is all about the other 6 1/2. The people who are currently cut off from international banking. What do you think happens when you suddenly are able to turn a simple text-messaging phone in the middle of a rural area in Nigeria, connected to a solar panel, into a bank terminal? Into a Western Union remittance terminal? Into an international loan-origination system? A stock market? An IPO engine? At first, nothing, but give it a few years.

We've seen what happens with the development of the cell-phone technology that was deployed in Africa faster than any other technology ever in the history of humanity. We see small villages, where they have no running water, wood fires to cook with, and no electricity — yet there's one little solar panel on top of a mud hut and that solar panel is not there for light. It's there to charge a Nokia 1000 feature phone. That phone gives them weather reports, grain prices at the local market, and connects them to the world. What happens when that phone becomes a bank? Because with bitcoin, it can be a bank. What happens when you connect 6 1/2 billion people to a global economy without any barriers to access?

> *"What happens when you connect 6 1/2 billion people to a global economy without any barriers to access?"*

# Remittances, Impacting Lives around the World

Bitcoin is not a currency. Bitcoin is the internet of money. As a technology, it can bring economic inclusion and empowerment to billions of people in the world. I'll give you one example of a specific application that is going to fundamentally change the lives of more than a billion people in the next five to ten years.

Every day, an immigrant somewhere cashes their paycheck and stands in line to wire 50 percent of that paycheck back to their home country to feed their extended family. Here in the US, 60 million people have no bank accounts, yet they cash their paychecks and send them abroad. Overall in the world, $550 billion is transmitted every year as remittances from first-world countries. Much of that money is sent to five major destinations: Mexico, India, the Philippines, Indonesia, and China. In some of these places, remittances represent up to 40 percent of the local economy. Sitting on top of that flow of $550 billion are companies like Western Union, and they take, on average, a cut of 9 percent of every single one of these transactions out of the pockets of the poorest people of the world.

> *"Imagine what happens when one day one of these immigrants figures out that they can send money back to their home country with bitcoin — not for 15 percent, not 10 percent, not 5 percent, but for 5 cents. Not a percentage; a flat fee."*

Imagine what happens when one day one of these immigrants figures out they can do the same thing with bitcoin — not for 15 percent, not 10 percent, not 5 percent, but for 5 cents. Not a percentage; a flat fee. What happens when they can do that? They can, right now. There is a startup company that is handling remittances between the US and the Philippines. They're doing a few million dollars right now, but they're going to start growing. There's $500 billion sitting behind that dam. When you're an immigrant and you can change your financial future by not paying 9 percent to send money home, imagine what happens if every month, instead of sending 91 dollars home, you send 100 dollars home. That makes a difference. There are a billion people, right now, with access to the internet and feature phones who could use bitcoin as an international wire-transfer service.

# Bitcoin Will Change the World

To sum up, bitcoin is the most exciting technology I have seen. I was on the internet in 1989 as a young kid. I knew it was going to change the world long before most people figured it out. I told everyone around me, "We're going to be shopping on this. We're going to do banking on this thing." People's reactions were quite predictable: "Yeah, Andreas, go do your homework, clean up your room." When I first saw Linux, I said, "Man, this is going to change operating systems forever. IBM is going down." Everybody laughed at me. When I saw the first web browser and the first website, I said, "Every single company in America is going to have a website within a decade." Everyone laughed at me. Well, let me tell you something.

I don't know what's going to happen with bitcoin, but I do know that the underlying invention — a system of digital currencies that has no banks, no governments, no central control and is available for anyone to use without asking permission — will change the world.

Thank you.

# Dumb Networks, Innovation, and the Festival of the Commons

*O'Reilly Radar Summit; San Francisco, California; January 2015*

Video Link: https://www.youtube.com/watch?v=x8FCRZ0BUCw

*At the beginning of the video, Andreas thanks O'Reilly for agreeing to publish his book, Mastering Bitcoin, under an open-source license. He thanks the audience and the entire community who helped write the book. It's available on github, Amazon, and at bitcoinbook.info*

Today, I want to talk about dumb networks. I want to talk about smart networks. I want to talk about the value of open source when it meets finance. And I want to talk about the festival of the commons.

> *"Bitcoin is a currency, a network, a technology. And you can't separate these things."*

Bitcoin is a currency. Bitcoin is a network. Bitcoin is a technology. And you can't separate these things. A consensus network that bases its value on currency does not work without the currency. You can't just do the blockchain without a valuable currency behind it, and the currency doesn't work without the network. Bitcoin is both. It is the convergence of a participatory consensus network and a global, borderless currency that is fungible, fast, and secure.

Today, I want to talk a bit about the bitcoin network and focus on one concept that has some parallels to the early internet.

## Smart vs. Dumb Networks

Bitcoin is not a smart network. Bitcoin is a dumb network. It really is a dumb network. It is a dumb transaction-processing network. It's a dumb network for verifying a very simple scripting language. It doesn't offer a complete range of financial services and products. It doesn't have automation and incredible features built in.

*"Bitcoin is simply a dumb network, and that is
one of its strongest and most important features."*

Bitcoin is simply a dumb network, and that is one of its strongest and most
important features. When you design networks, when you architect network
systems, one of the most fundamental choices is this: do you make a dumb network
that supports smart devices, or do you make a smart network that supports dumb
devices?

## The Smart Network - Phones

The phone network was a very smart network.   The telephone at the end of that
network was a very dumb device. If you had a pulse-dialing phone, that thing had
maybe four electronic components inside it. It was basically a switch on a wire
with a speaker attached to it. You could dial by flicking the hook up and down fast
enough.

The phone was a dumb device; it had no intelligence whatsoever. Everything
the phone network did was *in* the network. Caller ID was a network feature. Call
waiting was a network feature. And if you wanted to make the experience better,
you had to upgrade the network but you didn't need to upgrade the device. That was
a critical design decision because, at that time, the belief was that smart networks
were better because you could deliver these incredible services just by upgrading the
network for everyone.

*"As a result of smart network design, innovation
only happens when a feature is needed by all
of the subscribers of the network, when it is
compelling enough to disrupt the function of the
entire network to upgrade it."*

There is one small disadvantage with smart networks. They have to be upgraded
from the center out. And that means innovation occurs at the center, by one player,
and requires permission.  As a result of smart network design, innovation only
happens when a feature is needed by all of the subscribers of the network, when it is
compelling enough to disrupt the function of the entire network to upgrade it.

# The Dumb Network - Internet

The internet is a dumb network. It's dumb as rocks. All it can do is move data from point A to point B. It doesn't know what that data is. It can't tell the difference between a Skype call and a web page. It doesn't know if the device on the end is a desktop computer or a mobile phone, a vacuum cleaner, a refrigerator, or a car. It doesn't know if that device is powerful or not. If it can do multimedia or not. It doesn't know, it doesn't care.

> *"In order to run a new application or innovate on a dumb network, all you have to do is add innovation at the edge. Because a dumb network can support smart devices, you don't need to change anything in the network."*

In order to run a new application or innovate on a dumb network, all you have to do is add innovation at the edge. Because a dumb network can support smart devices, you don't need to change anything in the network. If you push intelligence to the edge of the network, an application that only has five users can be implemented so long as those five users upgrade their devices to implement that application. The dumb network will transport their data because it doesn't know the difference and it doesn't care.

## Bitcoin's Dumb Network

Bitcoin is a dumb network supporting really smart devices, and that is an incredibly powerful concept because bitcoin pushes all of the intelligence to the edge.

It doesn't care if the bitcoin address is the address of a multimillionaire, the address of a central bank, the address of a smart contract, the address of a device, or the address of a human. It doesn't know. It doesn't care if the transaction is carrying lots of money or not much money at all. It doesn't care if the address is in Kuala Lumpur or downtown New York. It doesn't know, it doesn't care.

It moves money from one address to another based on a simple locking script. And that means that if you want to build a new application on top of bitcoin, you can upgrade the devices and you can build an application. You don't need to ask for anyone's permission to innovate. Write the app, launch it on your endpoint, and bitcoin will route it, because bitcoin is a dumb network.

That is the power of innovation on the internet. It's innovation without permission. It's innovation without central approval. It's innovation without a broad network upgrade. And that means bitcoin is not a specific financial network. It's not a financial network for large transactions or small transactions, fast transactions or slow transactions. It's whatever you want to use it for, based upon what you choose to do at the endpoint.

Compare that to the current banking system. The current banking system is built around very smart networks, absolutely and tightly controlled to deliver very specific applications to very dumb endpoints. Even with your most sophisticated online banking, all you can do with your bank is access some HTML that delivers a set of services that they decided they were going to give you. You get no APIs, no ability to run additional applications, no ability to upgrade or innovate or change anything unless the entire network changes to support your new application. The current system has networks for large payments, small payments, or fast payments, but it's not all of the above. Bitcoin is all of those things because it's not discriminating, it's neutral, it doesn't care, it's dumb.

> *"The current system has networks for large payments, small payments, or fast payments, but it's not all of the above. Bitcoin is all of those things because it's not discriminating, it's neutral, it doesn't care, it's dumb."*

The power of pushing intelligence to the edge, of not making decisions in the center, moves the innovation into the hands of its end users and gives those end users the ability to build applications that are so niche that only a handful of people around the world need them. And they can build those applications without asking for anyone's permission.

# Tragedy of the Commons

But there's one more thing that's really unique about bitcoin, and it's one of the reasons that it continues to survive and continues to win over the centralized, closed networks of the past, and that is that bitcoin is open source, open standard, and open network.

One of the key concepts in economics is the idea of a tragedy of the commons. This is when you have a common resource that can be consumed, without limits, by all those who participate until the resource is depleted and the entire system collapses. It's a form of market failure called "the tragedy of the commons." The most common example of it is the commons, in the old British sense, of a large grassy area. Here you have a field that everyone can graze their cattle on, and if everybody goes and grazes their cattle with reckless abandon, before long, you have a big muddy pit and no cattle. Because everybody overgrazes it, the resource is depleted.

# Festival of the Commons

Bitcoin doesn't suffer from a tragedy of the commons like most financial networks do. I can't innovate on somebody else's network. When Visa innovates, only Visa wins. When MasterCard innovates, only MasterCard wins. If a feature is deployed on SWIFT, I don't get it as a consumer. If Bank of America makes something new and snazzy, they do it competitively and at the exclusion of every other bank that didn't implement that feature.

Bitcoin is a common resource whose use increases the value of that resource, at the exclusion of no one. If a company builds a new feature that can be used on bitcoin under an open-source license, that feature can then be used by everyone in the ecosystem. That means the innovation enriches everyone in the network. If a company invests money in bitcoin, the protocol, they benefit, but so does everybody else. When they play in the bitcoin sphere, they get to benefit from everybody else's investment in that space. So, it returns multiple times. You get this wonderful synergy where each company that invests in this amazing technology makes it better for everybody else. It's not an exclusionary principle; instead of a tragedy of the commons, you have a festival of the commons. A commons that gets better when more companies use it.

*"It's not an exclusionary principle; instead of a tragedy of the commons, in bitcoin you have a festival of the commons. A commons that gets better when more companies use it."*

## Festival of the Commons 2012-2014

Just look at some of the examples. 2014 was supposed to be the worst year in bitcoin. But that's only if you're focused on price, because in 2014 we saw the deployment of two incredible technologies. The first is multisig, which required a tiny change to the core protocol but then allowed an enormous amount of services and products to be built at the edge. The second is hierarchical deterministic wallets, which didn't require any changes to the core and allowed us to have these incredibly complex and rich experiences in the wallet space.

The companies that invented and deployed those two features did so in 2012 and we reap the benefits today. An entire ecosystem of new products and services have been built from those two inventions. The value invested by one company two years ago blows up and creates an entire range of products in a new industry two years later.

In 2014, during the worst year of bitcoin, 500 startups received $500 million in investment, generating tens of thousands of jobs, and none of that innovation has come back yet because they just started. All of the incredible technology advancements we saw in 2014 grew from inventions in 2012. Now, what happens when you throw 500 companies and 10,000 developers at the problem? Give us two years and you will see some pretty amazing things in bitcoin. And that is the advantage of the festival of the commons.

# Accelerating Innovation

While journalists are writing yet another obituary for bitcoin, I see an ecosystem of openness. I see an ecosystem that is generating jobs in an economy that is mostly dead. I see an ecosystem that has some of the smartest people I have ever met creating the most amazing innovations. And the really amazing thing about this is that we all benefit from all of this. We're not really competing against each other. We are participating in the festival of the commons, and as a result we're seeing a rate of innovation that is accelerating. It's already at breakneck speed, and it's accelerating.

Take an open, decentralized ecosystem with a festival of the commons — open source, open standards, open networking — and the intelligence and innovation pushed all the way to the edge so the users have control over what they innovate and how they invest their time and money and spirit into this technology. Put that against a closed system, controlled by a central provider, whose permission you need in order to innovate and who will only innovate at the exclusion and competition of all of the other companies. We will crush them.

People ask me, "Well, what happens if Goldman Sachs builds GoldmanSachsCoin?" I say, let them build it. If it's really open and decentralized, they just proved the whole point of this and we can all go home declaring victory. If it's closed and doesn't allow open innovation, it will become stagnant in just a few months while we continue accelerating ahead with more and more innovation feeding off each other's invention.

You cannot stop this. That's why I'm excited to be in the bitcoin space: a dumb network that puts all of the intelligence and innovation at the edge so that we can innovate without asking anyone's permission, and we can participate in this incredible festival of the commons.

Thank you.

# Infrastructure Inversion

*Zurich Bitcoin Meetup; Zurich, Switzerland; March 2016*

Video Link: https://www.youtube.com/watch?v=5ca70mCCf2M

Today, I'd like to talk about a concept that I like to call *infrastructure inversion*. I'm going to talk about how things change when a new technology must first use the old infrastructure, and how that creates a conflict, pressure that can lead to an infrastructure inversion.

## New Technologies, Riding on Old Infrastructure

Bitcoin is new. Bitcoin is different. When I use the term *bitcoin* here, I'm speaking broadly. What I'm talking about is decentralized network-centric platforms. These platforms can be used for currencies, payments, and other trust applications. The platform could be bitcoin, or something else. For this talk, I'll use the term *bitcoin* to cover that whole category that has now been created. It's new, and we're trying somehow to squeeze it on top of the existing banking system. The result is messy.

Not only is it messy, but it's also an opportunity for those who support the traditional banking system to say, "See, it's not working. It's slow. It doesn't work so well." This isn't new. This is a phenomenon that happens every time you have a new technology that is disruptive, that in the first few years of its adoption it has to be carried by the existing technology that it is disrupting.

> *"Every time you have a new technology that is disruptive, in the first few years of its adoption it has to be carried by the existing technology that it is disrupting."*

Let's take a historical look at how these things play out. When you read about a disruptive technology 20, 30, 40 years in the future, it is all very smooth. It's obvious because hindsight provides clarity. For example, automobiles were a great invention. And of course when automobiles were invented, everyone in the world said, "Yay! We don't need horses anymore." Right? That's not exactly what happened. Instead, they said, "That's crazy. Those noisy disgusting machines that are probably going to kill us all, they'll never work. And why would anyone other than stupid rich people playing with these crazy noisy toys want to use one of these horrible machines when we have perfectly good horses?"

This is what actually happens throughout history when you introduce a disruptive technology. You meet resistance. Resistance is the first reaction. The ones who succeed are the ones who continue—even though the rest of society tells them they're crazy—to pursue a crazy idea: automobiles, electrification, the internet, bitcoin. These crazy pioneers, who were made fun of by everyone else in society for their crazy ideas, persisted until everybody could see that what they were doing was correct.

## Infrastructure for Horses

Looking at that history, one of the really interesting things to me is that in the beginning, the disruptive technology has to live in a world created for the technology it's replacing. When you first ride your brand new automobile in a city, you are riding on roads used by horses with infrastructure designed and used for horses. There are no light signals. There are no road rules. There are no paved roads.

*"You are in horse society and you are the crazy one driving one of these horseless vehicles."*

There are a few things about horses that cars don't have. These early cars were forward-wheel drive. So, just two wheels turning. Horses are four-foot-drive vehicles, which gives them a lot of flexibility. They also have balance. You had a road that was designed for horses and it was not paved. Some of them had cobblestone, but the vast majority of roads were not paved. They were also not dry. They were usually covered in mud and horse poo (because that's what horses do). This is the environment that the automobile had to prove itself in. It didn't start out with "Yes, great, we have now invented an automobile. Allow me to demonstrate its capabilities on the Autobahn." Instead, the crazy rich people who were experimenting with this technology were driving their cars on roads with deep ruts, where the horses had been. On roads not designed for automobiles, in mud. And what happened? The cars got stuck because they didn't have balance and four feet.

The critics said, "Ha, we told you this is never going to work. Look at yourselves. You can't even get out of the mud. Also, where are you going to get gasoline? There is only one gasoline station. What happens if you run out of gasoline before you get there? I mean, if your horse gets hungry, you could at least go a few more miles, but if your new crazy car idea runs out of gasoline, that's it, you're stuck. You were already stuck because of the mud, but now you are really stuck because you ran out of gasoline. This is never going to work."

## From Horses to Vehicles

Often, new technology must first use the infrastructure of the technology it will eventually replace. In the beginning, automobiles had to use roads designed for horses. Eventually, we started paving roads. Then, something really interesting happened. When you pave roads and make them suitable for vehicles, the old technology (horses) can still use them. If you want to do a nice tour of Zurich on horseback, I am sure the horse would be perfectly comfortable. Horses are very comfortable on asphalt, as are skateboards, Segways, motorcycles, and bicycles — technologies that didn't exist. In fact, in order for those technologies to exist, you first had to build the infrastructure for automobiles.

Flat, paved roads not only allow the automobile to exist, allow the horse to comfortably exist, but they also open the door for new technologies. Now, you have people riding Segways, scooters, skateboards, rollerblades, pushing prams and all of the other things that are moving around on our streets.

That's an infrastructure inversion. You start with the new technology living on the old infrastructure and then, it flips. You build infrastructure and then the old infrastructure rides on top, on the infrastructure designed for the new technology.

*"That's an infrastructure inversion. You start with the new technology living on the old infrastructure and then, it flips."*

Let's look at more examples.

## Infrastructure for Natural Gas

One of the great things about history is that some of the most confident proclamations are often ridiculed for centuries because they are so ridiculous. For example, when electrification was introduced during the World's Fair in Paris, the mayor of Paris at the time said, "Electricity is a fad and as soon as we close the fair and take down the Eiffel Tower, electricity will vanish in history." Wrong on two counts. The Eiffel Tower is still standing and electrification won.

But think about the time when electrification was just beginning: there was no infrastructure. So how exactly do you put electricity into a home? First of all, the only reason to put electricity in the home is because you are one of those crazy rich people. Probably one of the same people that bought an automobile. You are now basically putting lightning in your walls, which is surely a crazy idea that will result in your house burning down. That's what the newspapers wrote. They wrote about every house that burned down and how these crazy people were putting electricity in their homes.

What was the infrastructure at the time? Back then, most of the infrastructure was designed to deliver gas. In fact, gas lighting in major cities was pretty common. There were pipes that could deliver gas primarily to street lights but also for home lights, as well as heating. You couldn't use that infrastructure for electricity. You couldn't use it to distribute electricity to homes.

At first, the only use for electricity was really for factories because that's where you could make the most use of electricity. Prior to electricity, a factory might have a very large gas-driven motor sitting in the corner of the factory. The motor distributed power through a series of belts and pulleys distributed throughout the factory to run all of the other equipment. It was basically a gas turbine. Electricity allowed you to distribute electricity directly to all of the equipment and use electric motors.

Obviously, factories could benefit from electricity, but why put it in your home? Why would you use electricity since you already had light and heating from gas and it worked fine? And there was no infrastructure. The infrastructure for gas wasn't useful for electricity. If you wanted it, you'd have to build new infrastructure.

Then we see the other aspect of this infrastructure inversion, which is that those invested in the status quo point to your new electricity projects and say, "There is not a large enough distribution network to create customers. And there are not enough customers to require a distribution network. This is never going to happen." Which is exactly what they said about cars. They said, "There are not enough gasoline stations to fill your cars and there are not enough customers to require gasoline stations. This will never happen."

## From Natural Gas to Electricity

Then, electrification starts happening, and people discover that once you put down electricity infrastructure, not only can you use that to do the new electricity capabilities, you can also use it to do the old applications. You can do light and heating and you can do them more effectively, in some cases, with electricity. But now, you can do new things. You can do fans and you can do air conditioning and you can do motors and you can do mixers and you can do hairdryers and, generally speaking, houses don't burn down because of electricity too often.

Again, we see infrastructure inversion. For the first few years, you have to run on the old infrastructure. It's almost impossible. You could theoretically attach a gas generator in your house and feed it with gas and generate electricity locally, but that wasn't very efficient. Then, you build infrastructure for the new technology, and that infrastructure enables the old technology quite comfortably—lighting, heating, or horses, in the case of roads. But it also opens the door for new applications that you couldn't do before. And the world changes.

*"Changing the infrastructure opens the door for new applications that you couldn't do before. And the world changes."*

## Infrastructure for Human Voices

My third example is a bit more technical. This is where you'll see the audience separate into those who are over 35 and those who are under 35. Tell me if you can recognize this sound.

*Andreas replicates the sound of a dial-up modem*

People under 35 are looking at me like I am crazy, and the people over 35 are saying, "That's a modem. I used to have one of those! That's how we connected to the internet." Forgive me as we go into ancient history. A modem is a modulator-demodulator. It's a device that speaks data over a telephone line. Here is the thing: if you think about it, the telephone line is like a dirt road and you're trying to drive a car over it.

A telephone line is a system designed to carry human voice. When I was a teenager, telephone lines were still analog and we had pulse dialing systems. We used to sometimes try to play music to our friends over the phone line. If you'd ever tried this, you would have discovered it didn't really work. The reason it didn't work is because the frequencies that a telephone line allows are very narrow.

You see, the telephone network is designed to do one thing and only one thing. It's highly specialized, just like the gas network that delivers gas to houses is only designed to deliver gas. Not water or electricity or oil. Just gas, and it's specialized. The telephone system was designed to deliver just voice, and human voice is very specific. Our main frequency is 1 kilohertz; we stay close to that range, sometimes going a bit above and a bit below. There are a few people who can go quite a bit beyond a common range. Teenagers can go to frequencies that I can't even hear anymore. But because of the specialized use of voice and because of the difficulties of transmitting voices, especially over great distances, engineers narrowed the acceptable range. If you allow a full range, you get voice but you also get static noises, electrical interference at very high frequencies. You also get humming noises, electrical interference from motors at very low frequencies. What happens if your phone line has static and humming noises? You add a filter that chops out the lows and another filter that chops out the highs. Now, the connection is cleaner but the human voice starts sounding weirder and weirder because it's being compressed.

This compressed road is a very difficult road to ride data over because when you're transmitting data, you need to get a lot of information into a very narrow frequency band. The whistling sound that you hear with the modem is actually two modems trying to test the available frequency range on this specific connection. All of those noises are the modems saying, in different frequencies, "Can you hear me now?" and the other saying, "I heard you. Can you hear me?" back and forth until the available range is established.

This is an insane way to do data transmission. You've basically got two devices that are singing to each other over a very narrow channel, trying to somehow squeeze as much data as possible through a narrow little straw. Then, we upgraded them and they got better and better at doing this.

The phone companies hated it: "That's not what we designed the networks for. This is a pristine, state-of-the-art voice-communicating network. What the hell are you people doing?" In fact, in the country where I grew up—in Athens, Greece— if you tried to make a long-distance call with the modem, what you would hear is the beginning of a modem connection and then an abrupt click. What? What just happened? They cut off the lines if they detected a modem. Why? Because it was competing against the phone company. Kind of like banks shutting down accounts of bitcoin companies. Or basically, exactly the same.

What did they say at the time? They said, "We could deploy data connections— fiber, coaxial cables, direct data connections at high bandwidths. But first of all, no one needs high bandwidth because what are they going to do? Transmit voice? We already have a voice network. It's fantastic. We don't need these new things. Secondly, you don't have enough users to deploy coax. And you don't have enough coax to build a user base. This is never going to happen." The same exact idea.

## From Voice to Data

Then, we had one of the most spectacular examples of infrastructure inversion that I have ever seen and that I recall from history. When, first, the internet was not wanted and carried over phone lines reluctantly. Then, the internet was carried over phone lines by phone companies becoming internet service providers. Then, gradually their backbones become data-oriented. Then, their entire network becomes digital. Then, their entire network starts running over the internet. Then, they start running all of their phone lines on top of the internet. Today, every single phone call you do anywhere in the world is carried over the internet, with a few exceptions at the edges in some developing countries. A complete infrastructure inversion.

*"Today, every single phone call you do anywhere in the world is carried over the internet, with a few exceptions at the edges in some developing countries. A complete infrastructure inversion."*

It turns out, it's very difficult to push data through a narrow phone line designed for voice, but if you flip the equation, putting voice over a data connection is trivially easy. What's the difference? One is extremely specialized. It had already chosen the application for you. The application is voice; data is the exception that you're trying to squeeze through. The other one is very generic. Data means anything, and voice is just one of the applications carried comfortably.

I think the ultimate irony for the phone companies was that special thing called "comfort noise generation." If you're a phone engineer, you know what I'm talking about. This is the most ironic thing ever. After years and years of people my age being used to their phone line having static all the time, when we started having cellular telephony and digital phone lines that were perfect, they had no noise. The moment the other person stopped talking, what you would have was complete silence. So, you were like "Oh, okay, I guess they hung up."

They didn't hang up. They were still there. There was just none of the static. Then, the phone companies invented the most brilliant technology ever, which is comfort noise generation. This is a device that sits on your end of the phone and it looks to see if the connection is still open, and if it is, it whispers static into your ear just to make you feel comfortable that the other person is still there. It actually generates high-frequency noise on purpose, artificially on your end—noise that isn't in the system, just so that you don't think the other person has hung up.

The very same companies that said, "We will never be able to do quality voice over the internet. We don't want the internet on our phone lines," are now injecting noise in order to simulate the terrible performance of the previous network because we're now delivering CD-quality or better sound across continents. Complete infrastructure inversion.

# From Banking to Bitcoin

Now, we have bitcoin. We have a decentralized trust platform that can do settlement of transactions on a global basis without intermediaries. But we're still living in the old system. Today, we have to use exchanges tied to traditional bank accounts, or use IBAN transfers, or credit cards. Today, we're riding the automobile along the muddy roads of banking. The bitcoin supercar, the Formula One of finance, is riding along on the muddy roads of 1970s mainframe-based banking, and it's a bumpy road.

> *"The bitcoin supercar, the Formula One of finance, is riding along on the muddy roads of 1970s mainframe-based banking, and it's a bumpy road."*

The banks point at this and say, "It's not working. Look, you have to do all of the regulation that we have to do. You have to do all of the identity that we have to do. You have to slow everything down to the speed of traditional banking. This is never going to work. Not only that, but you don't have enough users to build infrastructure, and you don't have enough infrastructure to attract new users. So, this is clearly never going to work."

But what we *do* have, just like with electricity and the automobile and the internet, is a new technology that has within it the promise of a thousand other applications they haven't even imagined.

I predict, over the next 15 to 20 years, we'll see a great infrastructure inversion happen in finance. First, the banks will resist. Then, the banks will adopt. The banks will run their systems alongside blockchain and bitcoin systems, and finally they will run all of traditional banking as an application on top of a decentralized trusted ledger. Because, while it is very hard to do a decentralized trusted ledger that's connected to all of these legacy banking systems, simulating legacy banking on top of a decentralized ledger, on top of bitcoin, an open global blockchain, is trivial. All you have to do is take all of its capabilities and slow them down. For example, I can create an application that takes your bitcoin transaction and makes it clear in three to five business days for a cost of 5 dollars. I have implemented traditional banking. It's kind of like comfort noise generation.

*"Over the next 15 to 20 years, we'll see a great infrastructure inversion happen in finance."*

For those of us so accustomed to the banking of a previous generation who say, "I don't like all of this fast finance. It makes me uncomfortable. I want to sit at my kitchen table every Sunday and balance my checkbook and make sure none of my checks bounced. I don't like all of this electronic instantaneous global transfer. It scares me," we can slow it down.

This infrastructure inversion will allow us to comfortably run traditional banking applications on top of a distributed global ledger — an open blockchain like bitcoin, *the* open blockchain, probably bitcoin's open blockchain and simultaneously open the door for other applications, for applications we've never seen before. These new applications will look different from traditional banking. As different as a Segway or skateboard looks to those committed to traditional horse-carriages. As different as moving to electricity in an era of gas lighting in traditional Victorian homes. As alien as comfort noise on high quality data voice communication over the internet that is capable of so much more.

Enabling the future on your legacy system is very difficult. While you're trying to do that, everyone is pointing at the future and saying, "Look. It doesn't work." Once you flip the infrastructure, simulating the past on the network of the future becomes extremely easy.

*"Once you flip the infrastructure, simulating the past on the network of the future becomes extremely easy."*

What we're part of now is the very early stages as we look at the future of money, and the first stages of the greatest infrastructure inversion the world has ever seen.

Thank you.

# Currency as a Language

*Bitcoin Expo 2014 - Keynote; Toronto, Ontario, Canada; April 2014*

Video Link: https://www.youtube.com/watch?v=jw28y81s7Wo

This is going to be a bit more of a philosophical talk about the future of cryptocurrencies and what I've learned here at this event. This event is called the Bitcoin Expo 2014. It might have been called the Bitcoin and Ethereum Expo 2014. I don't know if you noticed, but Ethereum had a pretty big presence here. An interesting question comes up, actually quite a few people have asked me: "Does Ethereum threaten the future of bitcoin? Does it steal some of its thunder?" Those are questions I've heard several times, and I've heard people refer to that issue in trying to understand altcoins — wondering whether altcoins essentially threaten the dominance of bitcoin, if they make bitcoin weaker, if they distribute the value of the network too broadly.

## Born into Currency

I've been thinking about this question for quite a while. I think, fundamentally, it's a question that evokes the old paradigm of currencies. We've all grown up in a world where currencies are forced upon us in a monopolistic fashion, where currencies are defined strictly by the geographies in which they occur, and where the choice of currency is not yours. It is an accident of birth, just like many other things in our lives. As an accident of birth, I was born into an upper-middle-class family in Greece, fully loaded with a lottery of privilege in my life. I also acquired the drachma. I didn't choose the drachma any more than I chose to be a white male, any more than I chose to be born into a family of educated people. Those things simply happened to me.

> *"Currency is an artifact of the nation-state. It imposes upon us a certain constraint. We don't choose our currency; it chooses us."*

Currency, as we understand it, is an artifact of the nation-state. It imposes upon us certain constraints. We don't choose our currency; it chooses us. We are forced to use that currency in all of our interactions. We don't have a choice — until 2008, that is. We now live in a slightly different world, but a lot of the old paradigm persists in our thinking.

In a world where your currency is a monopolistic nation-state artifact that is constrained by geography, it's a zero-sum game. The currency is the flag, is the nation-state. It is the expression of the economic value of your state. It defines your interactions in a world of geopolitics, in a global struggle for domination among nations. It's not up to individual choice. It has nothing to do with the individual, except for that one individual whose face is on the currency — up until recently here in Canada, some old white lady named Elizabeth.

## Currency as a Means of Expression

Now, we live in a new world, a world in which currency is a choice, and not just a choice in terms of use. It's not just a matter of being able to choose which currency we use as individuals. It's also a means of expression. Any of us can now create a currency using a simple web form.

> *"Now, we live in a new world, a world in which currency is a choice, and not just a choice in terms of use… It's also a means of expression."*

As I thought about the evolution of alt-currencies, as they're called, I realized I was asking the wrong questions. How many currencies will there be? How many altcoins will there be? How will altcoins compete in a world of cryptocurrencies as we move into the future? Will there be hundreds of altcoins? If there are hundreds of altcoins, what does that mean for the value of each of the altcoins? How do they compete? That was the wrong way of thinking about it. I saw currency as a zero-sum game, just like it had been imposed on my worldview from the nation-states that created currency. Then, I started thinking of currency as an application. And then, I started thinking of currency as a means of expression.

You see, money, at the very root of it, is a language. It's a language we use to express value to each other. When I give you a dollar bill, I am saying that I want to hand you the equivalent value. I'm communicating my desire to exchange value with you, because I appreciate something you can do or something you can give to me. I'm using money as a token of language.

*"Money, at the very root of it, is a language. It's a language that we use to express value to each other. When I give you a dollar bill, I'm saying that I want to hand you the equivalent value. I'm communicating my desire to exchange value with you."*

## Inventing Currency on the Playground

This happens in human societies whether you have formal currencies or not. If you don't have a currency with a stamped face on it, you invent it. One of the things that really captivated me was understanding that if you have a primary-school environment and you watch children in their natural habitat (a very unnatural habitat in most schools), young children don't have currency, and they don't understand currency. But they invent currency. They start trading. Rubber bands, Pokemon cards, Tamagotchi, tokens of affection, tokens of popularity. Humans create currency as a means of expressing their desires, of expressing their individuality. I thought, What happens when a five-year-old in a primary school can use a website to create Joeycoin to compete against Mariacoin in a game of popularity within their school?

Then it dawned on me: To ask the question, "How many currencies will exist?" is equivalent to asking the question, "How many bloggers will there be on the internet?" The answer is simple: all of us.

Currency is now a means of expression. But if everyone can create a currency, how does it derive value and what does it mean? What is the difference between currency as an expression of popularity, as an expression of desire, as a meme, a fad, a brand? Down there right now, *Andreas points outside of auditorium*, a Canadian teen idol contest is running. One of those contestants, Amir, has a big fan group. Maybe he wants to create AmirCoin so that his fans can express their desire to watch more of his dancing. Why not? People have talked about me doing AndreasCoin. I think it's a bit silly. But, why not? I think at some point we're going to see things like that happen.

We're not going to have hundreds of altcoins. We're not going to have thousands of altcoins. We're going to have hundreds of thousands, and then millions of altcoins. Then, there will be thousands of altcoins being created every day to organize local communities to express fads, to create popularity contests, to codify the latest internet meme.

*"We're not going to have hundreds of altcoins.
We're not going to have thousands of altcoins.
We're going to have hundreds of thousands, and
then millions of altcoins."*

# Authority by Production

With so many altcoins, how do you tell which ones have value and which ones
don't? In order to try to answer these types of questions, I often reflect on the
emergence of the first decentralized system in my lifetime, the internet. What it
did for understanding information, information scarcity, opinion, and authority of
opinion. What it did to us as a society as the internet emerged into our global scene.

There used to be a time when if you wanted to read authoritative opinion, you
bought a piece of paper from an organization that had a printing press that was
three stories high and four football fields long and had a really great name, like *The
New York Times*. That organization could buy ink by the barrel, and through that
ownership of this enormous manufacturing facility, they had the weight of authority.
We imbued authority into these institutions, and we used that authority to decide
which opinions mattered and which opinions didn't. We used them as gatekeepers
of authority to give us guidance in understanding opinion.

Then, the internet destroyed all of that, because suddenly *anyone* could print,
*anyone* could publish.

# Authority by Merit

In the early days, people asked, "How will we know which opinions matter if
anyone can have an opinion?" The world will come to an end, they thought. But
a funny thing happened. We shifted from a world in which authority and opinion
came from the issuer, from the authority of the publisher by proxy, into a world
where we had to look at opinion on its own merits, on the content of that opinion.
We arrived at a world where *The New York Times* prints bullshit that sends an entire
nation into war, and an Egyptian blogger on the front lines of a revolution prints the
truth that nobody wants to hear. Suddenly, the world is upside down. Authority is no
longer the person who owns the printing press. Now the person who has the content
is what matters. We just did this to currency.

*"Authority is no longer the person who owns the printing press. Now the person who has the content is what matters."*

# Valuing Currencies by Use

Now, the authority is not derived from the sovereignty of the issuer, from the printing press of a nation-state that can declare through monopoly and use of force that this is the currency you will use. Now, we can choose currency, and a five-year-old can create currency. Maybe the currency that the five-year-old created has monetary value, maybe it doesn't. Most likely, it doesn't. But some will. We need to get used to a world where we have to judge currency not by who issued it, but by who uses it. Or rather, by how many people use it and what they use it for.

*"We need to get used to a world where we have to judge currency not by who issued it, but by who uses it. Or rather, by how many people use it and what they use it for."*

Let's imagine a world in which a currency is being used in a widespread fashion, and no one remembers who created the currency or why. They only know that within their local community, it has purchasing power. As a little fanciful thought: Imagine a decade from now, in a rural village detached from developed nations, villagers exchanging two currencies. One has a Shiba Inu, a Japanese breed of dog, on the front and is pronounced *Dogecoin*. I'm not quite sure how to pronounce it and it doesn't really matter, but you can buy half a dozen eggs with it. The other villagers are trading another currency that has an old white lady named Elizabeth on it. They have no idea who Elizabeth is. They don't know why she got her picture on the coin. Maybe she wrote a nice song. Maybe she won Canadian *Teen Idol*. Nobody remembers anymore, but you can buy six eggs with it.

To those people, it doesn't matter who issued the currency; what matters is whether it has purchasing power or not. The currency is now evaluated purely on its monetary basis, because of adoption, because of use. There is one fundamental difference between those two currencies. One has a predictable, stable, algorithmic monetary supply. The other has an old white lady named Elizabeth on it. So, in fact, one of them has some real intrinsic value because it has removed some of the uncertainty of the monetary system from it. The other one doesn't really.

We need to get ready to live in a world where multiple currencies will coexist.

## Multiple Currencies Coexist

Currency as a means of expression, currency as a tool of language, is no longer up to the issuer. It is up to us as individuals making a choice to use that currency, and we give it value through our use. We give it value through adoption. We will be surprised by some of the currencies that will emerge from a fad, a joke, perhaps even a sick joke, and will explode into viral consciousness on the internet and then become real monetary powers in use across a broad population.

How do we operate in that kind of world? What does it mean to have competition between currencies if there are millions? What if digital scarcity really applies, but only on a local basis and only in the context of each of these currencies? What if scarcity is not derived from the issuer but is derived in terms of adoption and in terms of the token itself?

> *"Currency as a means of expression, currency as a tool of language, is no longer up to the issuer. It is up to us as individuals making a choice to use that currency, and we give it value through our use."*

We're going to have currencies for different uses. Already, you have bitcoin that provides a very specific monetary policy. You have Ethereum that can provide a contract platform. There's Namecoin for distributed naming conventions. There are many others, and there will be many others that will solve other problems: protein folding, the search for extraterrestrial life. Maybe we'll have currencies that are better for microtransactions and micropayments with very fast resolution. Maybe we'll have currencies that are better for larger transactions, like real estate. Who knows. If you think of currency as an application, then you realize that it doesn't really matter.

On the internet, email was the granddaddy of them all. Or the grandma of them all. Email, like bitcoin, was the killer app that allowed us all to see the power of decentralized communications and adopt this new platform. It was enough to create utility to spread this network all around the world, but it was only the first app. Then, instant messaging, forums, bulletin boards, Facebook, Twitter. Do you worry that Twitter will destroy email? Do you worry that Facebook will destroy instant messaging? Do you worry that the value of email is eroded somehow by the existence of Twitter? We don't worry about these things because we understand that each one serves a different purpose. Some allow us to express a modality of instantaneous, real-time communication. Some allow us to have asymmetric communication, where using Twitter I can address an audience of thousands and receive real-time feedback without having to have a bi-directional, synchronous communication. Some, like email, allow us to have more long-term, asynchronous communication between people.

What we do is we build interfaces, we build abstractions, we build unifying tools that allow us to use all of these modalities from a single interface and fluidly move from one to the other. So, we can start transmitting a short text message to someone, get into a conversation, convert that to an audio conversation, decide that we want to show them our dog, turn on the video camera, convert it into a video conference, and when we're finished with the conversation, follow up with an email to summarize what we've agreed on. Now we've gone through five different modalities of communication in a single unified interface.

> *"What we do is we build interfaces, we build abstractions, we build unifying tools that allow us to use all of these modalities from a single interface and fluidly move from one to the other."*

## Currency as an App

I think that's what's going to happen with currency. We're going to start treating currency as an application, and in order to do that we're going to need interfaces that allow us a unified currency experience, that allow us to have a single wallet with perhaps 150 different currencies in it. Because of inventions like sidechains, decentralized exchanges, fluid liquid systems and the complete absence of monopoly, of lock-in, of hostage situations around the currency, we will be able to instantaneously and at very low cost convert from bitcoin to Namecoin to Dogecoin to Ethereum. If we can do that, then it doesn't matter because *we* won't do that; our unified wallet interface will do that, by trying to see what we're trying to achieve with our currency. If I'm buying a house, it might express my transactional will in the modality of bitcoin because that is the most suitable currency. When I try to name the domain for that house, it will convert some to Namecoin. The contract itself will be paid in ether. When I tip the bartender for the cup of coffee they gave me when I got up that morning, I'll tip them in Doge. My interface will hide all of these differences.

> *"We're going to start treating currency as an application, and in order to do that we're going to need interfaces that allow us a unified currency experience, that allow us to have a single wallet with perhaps 150 different currencies in it."*

I can see a world in which we can smoothly move between currencies in a multimodal way. There's one other thing that comes out of this, which is the very real possibility that we will abstract value in exchange rate from the actual currency. If we have a multimodal communication system, we no longer need to look at the individual values and exchange rates of all of these commodities, assets, currencies, call them whatever you want.

## Index Currency

There's a very real possibility we're going to have an index currency: a currency that is not in itself tradable, that has no intrinsic use as a transactional commodity, but instead is only used to express the purchasing power vis-à-vis the various coins in our wallets.   I may have a thousand unified currency units. You can't buy unified currency units. You can buy bitcoin and then you can tell me how many unified currency units that is. I price everything in unified currency units, and then I pay in Dogecoin or Namecoin or bitcoin or Ether, depending on how I want to use it.

> *"I can see a world in which we can smoothly move between currencies in a multimodal way."*

We already do this in financial markets. In fact, you can trade S&P 500. You're not buying a single company; what you're buying into is the aggregation of all of the different things that are in the stock market as an expression of the total value of the market. You can then use that meta-instrument in order to price transactions.

For example, the London Interbank Offered Rate is used as a meta-interest rate to contractually tie things to a global set of interest rates. You don't need to say, "I will buy this at whatever the Bundesbank says." You say, "I'll buy this at LIBOR plus 2," and then you have a stable point of reference for transactions.

I expect we're going to see much of the same with currency. We're probably going to see meta-currencies whose only purpose is to aggregate the value in all of our wallets for all of our currencies, and allow us to understand value as an abstraction that exists independently of the currencies in which it's expressed.

# Choosing Currencies and Communities

So, that's a slightly philosophical perspective. That's why I think it doesn't matter: Ether is not competing with bitcoin; bitcoin is not competing with Litecoin. They are all means to express the transactional modality we want to use at any point in time to achieve our goals. With this comes a very important and powerful tool. In the choices we make with these currencies, we are also choosing to align ourselves with a community.

*"Adoption is not simply the act of using the currency; it's also attaching oneself to a community that has also chosen to adopt that currency."*

Adoption is not simply the act of using the currency; it's also attaching oneself to a community that has also chosen to adopt that currency. When I choose to adopt bitcoin, I am a believer in a monetary policy of 21 million total coins as a stable source of value. If I choose to adopt Freicoin, I am a believer in an inflationary-basis, demurrage coin that has a negative interest rate, that enforces consumption and discourages hoarding. I am choosing my politics through my currency, and through that choice I am associating myself with a global community that has made the same choice as me, and that is expressing that choice through currency. Just like when I choose an application on the internet to communicate with, I'm also aligning myself with a corresponding community. I don't use Twitter just because it's a convenient communication mechanism. I use Twitter because I also agree with many of the concepts and philosophies of the community of other people who choose to use Twitter.

With currency, that choice is a much more powerful political choice. We have entered the realm of meta-politics, of politics by algorithm, of the ability for global communities to form around a common consensus of politics through the choice of currency.   You want inflation? Use an inflationary currency. You're a goldbug? Use a deflationary currency. You want a currency that creates a guaranteed minimum income for the poor? Use a currency that expresses those politics. You want a currency that puts aside tokens for carbon sequestration? Use a currency that expresses your green politics. We're going to start seeing communities, politics, and currencies converge and allow us to make these choices. Just like I can support Joeycoin in order to say that Joey is in fact the coolest kid among the five-year-olds, I can support Greencoin because I care about global warming. Or not. I can support Meatcoin if I really really like red meat. Whatever. WorldWideWrestlingCoin, no problem. There'll be one of those, too.

Really, all of these things are forms of expression, and that comes back to the original point: that currency, in the end, is really a form of language. It's a language by which we communicate our expectations and desires of value, and now that we can do it on such a massive scale, now that everyone can create currency, our choices will really matter. We're past the zero-sum game. This isn't about nation-states anymore. This isn't about who adopts bitcoin first or who adopts cryptocurrencies first, because the internet is adopting cryptocurrencies, and the internet is the world's largest economy. It is the first transnational economy, and it needs a transnational currency.

# Currency Creates Sovereignty

To summarize, we've inverted the very basic and most fundamental equation of currency. For millenia, until the year 2008, sovereignty defined currency. Sovereignty was the basis upon which currency could be created, and that currency allowed that sovereignty to be expressed. The monopolistic control of currency is the basis of sovereignty. Now, the internet has a currency. The internet is going to use that currency to create sovereignty.

*"After 2008, currency creates sovereignty."*

After 2008, currency creates sovereignty. The internet has its own currency, which means that the internet has purchasing power. Which means the internet has economic freedom. Which means the internet can exert that economic freedom in a post-nationalist way, in a way that ignores borders and makes the nation-state not obsolete, but simply less relevant. When an Egyptian blogger can not only blog about the revolution but also fund that revolution in bitcoin, and they can connect with people from all around the world who share their ideas for self-determination and freedom, they are expressing their own sovereignty as an individual, and they are expressing the sovereignty of their community through the use of that currency.

This is the world we now live in: a world in which currencies can coexist, and where currency and its user adoption create sovereignty.

Thank you.

# Bitcoin Design Principles

*This talk was delivered in June 2015 at the Harvard Innovation Lab in Boston, Massachusetts, as part of an IDEO Lab design workshop. During this two-day workshop, students competed to create prototype applications based on bitcoin and blockchains.*

Video Link: https://www.youtube.com/watch?v=Ur037LYsb8M

Good morning, everyone. Wow, what a difficult task you have. At a very basic level, you have to try to understand *what is bitcoin*. I can answer that question in four words. Bitcoin is digital money. But that doesn't really capture it. It's more like the internet of money. But really it's a consensus decentralized network based on blockchain technology and a proof-of-work algorithm that allows a digital token to act as a reward system for a game-theoretical competition between decentralized miners who validate—and "Oh my...," it immediately goes off the cliff.

Even after a couple of years of exploring "What is bitcoin?" you'll find you're still learning, you're still trying to understand what it is. Part of the reason for that is because bitcoin is a really new technology, it's a really disruptive technology, but it also is an abstraction on a technology that is really old. That technology is money. Money is a tool, it's a technology. It actually shares commonalities with linguistic structures, because we use it almost like a language to communicate value among ourselves in a society.

## History of Money

Who wants to tell me here how old money is? *Audience member: "5,000?"* Okay, that's a good guess. A bit older. Try again. The problem with trying to understand the history of money is that money is older than history. We can go and look at the writing about money. Money is older than writing. That may confuse you a bit. You're like, "Money's older than writing? That can't be." In fact, if you look at the first forms of writing that we can find, they are spreadsheets. They are accounting ledgers. The first thing scratched onto tablets created with twigs and things like that are accounting ledgers. They represent how many amphorae of oil were given to the pharaoh. If you go even further back, we find ancient forms of money among the ruins of ancient civilizations: beads, feathers, shells, giant stones. Money has taken many forms, but it exists and has existed almost as long as language. This is a truly ancient technology. So, it's not 5,000 years. It's probably close to 500,000 years old.

## Primates and Money

In fact, we see money emerge within other species. Highly intelligent species like primates, certain types of birds like crows, even marine mammals like dolphins have forms of tokens that they use to express value to each other. Or they can very quickly learn the mechanics of money. You can teach primates that if you turn in this pebble, you get a banana. And then watch, within a very short period of time, how that not only becomes a part of the primate culture but gets passed down to the next generation, and they start inventing economic activities. Not nice economic activities. They invent strong-armed robbery: beat up the other monkey and take its pebbles, so you can get bananas. They invent sexual favors for pebbles, so you can get bananas. They invent some of the earliest economic activities.

*"Highly intelligent species like primates, certain types of birds like crows, even marine mammals like dolphins have forms of tokens that they use to express value to each other."*

Money is ancient, it's an absolutely ancient technology, and none of us really understands it. If you want a demonstration of that fact, sit down and have a conversation with a four-year-old and try to explain money. You'll find out very quickly that the four-year-old has very good questions that you can't answer. You can watch parents go through this, it's hilarious:

"Mommy, where does money come from?" "The banks make it." "How do they make it?" "Well, they print it." "Why can't we have more, then." "Go clean your room."

You're about four questions from "Go clean your room" in a money conversation because adults don't really understand money. Even though it is a cultural artifact that has existed in our species for hundreds of thousands of years, we don't understand how it works.

# Characteristics of Money

We've gone through several technological iterations of money. We started with very basic forms of money. These basic forms had certain unique characteristics that made them good as money. What makes good money? Something that is rare. Shells, feathers. You can use shells as money, unless you live on a beach; if you live on a beach, you can't use shells as money. You can transport the value easily. So, it has to be portable. With few exceptions, most forms of money are highly portable. If the amount of money you need to go to buy a cow is heavier than the cow, that's not very good money. Which is why we don't often see, for example, gold being used for large transactions. It's too heavy. Other characteristics of money . . . It has to be difficult to forge; it has to be difficult to create more of it. You should be able to detect at a glance or relatively easily that it is real. It should be fungible. If I'm using shells, then this shell or that shell are both the same money. If I give you a dollar, it doesn't matter which dollar I gave you; it's fungible. Every dollar can substitute for every other dollar.

> *"Money itself is an abstraction. If it's not an abstraction, then it's not money—it's barter."*

These are the technologies, and gradually over time we've created abstractions. Money itself is an abstraction. If it's not an abstraction, then it's not money—it's barter. If I give you bananas for your goat, that's not money. Bananas are not money because you eat them. You don't use them to do further exchanges. Therefore, that's barter. You're exchanging one commodity for another. If it's abstract—if it doesn't have any practical use in itself—then as an abstraction of money it represents something else, some shared value.

Which leads to the one inescapable conclusion about money: Money is a shared cultural hallucination. It's a shared delusion. We walk around and associate with other people on the basis of germ-ridden pieces of cotton printed with green ink. If you were to observe that as an alien anthropologist that landed on Earth, you'd think it was very very weird. That just by exchanging these pieces of cotton, you could create social relationships, transactions, and trade— you could feed yourself, shelter yourself, etc., etc. It doesn't make much sense but it's based on a shared hallucination. It's based on the assumption that if you give me a dollar today, someone else will accept that dollar in exchange for something of value tomorrow. If I still believe that is the case, then it has value. Value comes from the assumption that I can use it again.

> *"Money is a shared cultural hallucination."*

## Just Another Abstraction of Money

Bitcoin is just the latest iteration of abstraction. We've done abstraction before but every time we do abstraction of money, society freaks out because this new thing can't possibly be real money. Go back and look at what happened with the introduction of coins stamped onto nonprecious metal, and then eventually paper notes. When paper notes were first circulated, no one believed that they had value. The shared hallucination had not taken hold yet. It was very difficult to persuade people to exchange real gold coins or silver coins for pieces of paper that said that they had gold in a vault. Then, take it a step further, and disappear the gold from the vault and say, "Turns out, it's just the paper."

> *"...every time we do abstraction of money,*
> *society freaks out because this new thing can't*
> *possibly be real money."*

You ask people about bitcoin, and one of the first things I hear from most people is that it's not real money because it's not backed by gold like the US dollar—which I find astonishing. The dollar hasn't been backed by gold since 1936. Yet, most people think that somewhere in the vault, possibly at Fort Knox or some other movie location, there are bars of gold that correspond ingot to ingot to the pieces of paper that you have in your pocket. They don't. There's no such thing. Why is bitcoin money? Because other people think it's money. You can write a dozen Ph.D. dissertations explaining exactly why bitcoin is not money . . . and I have lived on it for two years. Therefore, it doesn't matter what your dissertation says. To me, it is money, *because* I have lived on it for two years. So have thousands of other people. Therefore, to me, it is very much real money.

# Bitcoin and Design

You've been tasked with creating designs and concepts around the oldest technology in the world that very few people really understand. Its latest, most abstract expression, that is brand new, is completely disjointed from previous expressions of money and is extremely complex as a technology. That is a really difficult task. When faced with that task, your go-to technique is the use of metaphor. Design metaphors are extremely powerful tools. They allow us to create expectations. Metaphors are tools by which we create expectations. When you have a desktop computer and it has a desktop, you assume that something will happen when you drag something across the desktop. Because you've actually used a real desk, that assumption will inform your expectations. You expect it to behave like the object that it's pretending to be. That's a design metaphor. Design metaphors are extremely powerful, but they're also extremely dangerous when misapplied.

> *"Design metaphors are extremely powerful, but they're also extremely dangerous when misapplied. In bitcoin, every single term and design metaphor is wrong and broken."*

## Wallets Aren't Wallets

In bitcoin, every single term and design metaphor is wrong and broken. Let's go through the list. You've probably struggled with this as you've engaged with this technology of bitcoin and looked at all of the terminology. First of all, a "wallet." What is a wallet? A wallet is something that stores money. Not in bitcoin it isn't. The money isn't in the wallet; the money is on the network. The wallet contains keys. So, it's not a wallet; it's a keychain. How can you tell it's not a wallet? Can you copy a wallet? No. But you can copy a key. A keychain is a far better metaphor. If I have a keychain—imagine a big ring of keys like a janitor or a custodian—I have a bunch of keys, and I can go into a shop and have all of those keys duplicated and create a second keychain. Both of those keychains will work interchangeably in all of the locks that the original keychain worked. That's how a keychain works. If you understand what a keychain does, then you will understand how a bitcoin wallet works. You can copy it, you can make copies of the keys. If you give someone a copy of the key, they can open the door. They don't need your permission anymore to open the door.

So, a "wallet" is not a wallet; it's a keychain. That's a terrible metaphor. You have expectations of what a wallet will do. It will contain things. These contents will be discrete and enumerated. None of that exists in bitcoin.

## No Coins in Bitcoin

Let's get down to basics: "Bit - coin." *Coin.* What a terrible word. What a terrible brand. *Coin.* Take the most abstract form of money we have ever created, that is based on a completely decentralized network that has no coins, and then name it "bitcoin." Just to confuse everyone. A coin, which is two generations of technology back and a far less abstract, much more tangible, physical representation of money. You took the most abstract representation of money and named it after the most tangible representation of money. Only an engineer could come up with that brand.

Here's a little secret: there are no coins in bitcoin. When miners mine, they don't create coins; they create ledger entries. Those ledger entries do not enumerate coins. They have outputs—transaction outputs—which are chunks of value that are infinitely divisible and recombinable. Coins don't do that. You can't track a coin in bitcoin because there are no coins.

So, you've got a "wallet" that doesn't contain "coins"—because the coins are actually on the network and they're not coins, they're outputs—and what you're really holding is a keychain. Transactions are not from a sender to a recipient. Addresses don't have balance in bitcoin. There's no such thing as a balance of an address. An address controls outputs, and if you trawl through the blockchain and add up all of the outputs, you can figure out some notional balance. Whether that's actually spendable or not, how much it is, is actually quite difficult to determine. There is no "balance." You have no "account" in bitcoin.

All of the terms are broken. The problem is, from a design perspective, instead of the metaphor informing our expectations, it is misinforming our expectations. It is creating the grounds for massive misunderstanding, because we think it's going to do something in a certain way, and it ends up doing something completely different, something unexpected. Kind of like the Windows desktop. I don't know if you've ever compared a Mac and a Windows desktop. To me Windows desktops have no consistency. The metaphor is completely broken. You expect it to do one thing, it does something completely different and confuses. The essence of good design is picking the metaphor that informs expectations.

> *"The essence of good design is picking the metaphor that informs expectations."*

# Skeuomorphic Design

Here's the next big problem with metaphors and design. There's a certain concept called *skeuomorphic design*. The word *skeuomorphic* means "a shadow of its former self." It's form as a shadow. What it means is when you create elements in design that give you references or hints of some previous form. For example, a classic example, in the first iteration of iPads, the iOS software had a lot of skeuomorphic design. If you opened your contact database, it was bound in leather. That leather had stitching. That stitching didn't do anything. It was just a design element which had no functional purpose, whose intent was to put you into a familiar set of mind so that you could understand the metaphor. When you're playing a card game on your computer and it has fake felt under the cards, that's because it's trying to draw out the metaphor of a casino by introducing this design element. Skeuomorphic design is extremely powerful. It's also extremely dangerous. If you don't use it correctly, again, it creates different expectations as to what is going to happen next.

In bitcoin, we have a lot of skeuomorphic design. My favorite and most hated form of skeuomorphic design is the picture you will see in every single article written about bitcoin: a pile of gold coins with a letter B on them, usually the Casascius coin designed by Mike Caldwell, but possibly some other rendering of that. Taking the worst design metaphor of bitcoin, the word "coin," and then instantiating it in a beautiful rendering that makes it even more physical looking, in a skeuomorphic design that completely misleads everyone. People are actually going out on eBay and they're buying what they think is "bitcoin." They're buying gold-plated, physical coins that have nothing to do with the blockchain but have the letter B stamped on them. "Look, I've joined the revolution of digital money" they say, but these tangible replicas rarely have any value in bitcoin. This is the result. Then, people write articles, and they look at the picture and they think, "So that's what a bitcoin looks like." That's not what a bitcoin looks like, because if you remember, I may have mentioned, there are no coins. This is the danger.

# Designing for Innovation

It's a really difficult task to design good metaphors for bitcoin because there is no parallel. We have never done this before. We fall into these traps of trying to extrapolate from our previous experience, and fall short. Disruptive technologies do this. In an incremental technology, if you take what you currently understand and then just use a milligram of vision and extend it just a tiny bit, you understand the new technology because it really is just a slight extension of the past. Bitcoin is a radical break from the past, so understanding the way traditional money works doesn't help you understand bitcoin. If anything, it hinders your understanding of bitcoin. The people who understand bitcoin the least are monetary economists. They cannot wrap their heads around it. They will write long theses on how bitcoin is not money, despite the fact that I've been living on it for years.

> *"Bitcoin is a radical break from the past, so understanding the way traditional money works doesn't help you understand bitcoin."*

Understanding disruptive technologies is even harder than understanding incremental technologies because the most interesting things they do have no previous parallel. Think about it this way . . . Look back at *Star Trek* in the 1970s.

What did they get right? They got tricorders. They got portable communicators. They got video telephony. They got all that was predictable with the technology of the 1970s. They couldn't possibly get the internet. They couldn't possibly understand the idea of networked information stores. They had fantastical computers that could talk to you, but they didn't have access to any data. They couldn't possibly predict things like social media. Most importantly, if you pay attention, you will notice something very strange. *Star Trek* doesn't have any money at all. There is no money anywhere in the *Star Trek* universe. Why is that? Because their furthest vision of the possibility of society is a society without money, a society without a language for transmitting value, which is probably the most radical departure from reality.

## Predicting the Future

When we try to predict the future, there are certain areas that are completely dark to us. These are the areas that have never been seen before. These are the applications that we cannot imagine because, in order for them to come into being, many things have to fall into place. For the web to happen, you needed a common standardized transmission protocol. For the web to give birth to social media, you needed massive penetration of basic email and TCP/IP connections. You needed penetration of those connections on an always-on state. You needed to have mobile devices with high-density computing in the palm of your hand that were internet connected. All of those things had to come to fruition before social media was even possible.

> *"If you look at the internet in 1992, you think that it will replace the phone. That's the only experience that you have."*

If you look at the internet in 1992, you think that it will replace the phone. That's the only experience that you have. The internet is a fancy phone. Perhaps it's a fancy phone/fax, perhaps a multifunctional printer/fax/phone. It's very fancy. So, the phone companies look at this and say, "Oh, it's a fancy phone. We can do this." They were wrong, fortunately. Otherwise, every time I went on a Skype call, there would be a little slot on the side of my computer, and I would have to deposit quarters every three seconds to make a Skype call. Fortunately, the phone companies didn't get to write the rules. They couldn't possibly predict the outcomes we saw on the internet, because most of the interesting things were not incremental improvements or extensions of the things before. They were radical departures from the past, because they created the conditions for things that were not possible before.

Let's go back to bitcoin and think about this for a second. Consider what we've been talking about: financial transactions, banking, payments. "It's a fancy credit card." "It's Paypal, basically. It's a global Paypal." But it's not. It's something completely, radically different, but we can't see where that's going to go. The applications that are going to happen on bitcoin, the really interesting applications, are those that can only happen when you have sufficient adoption and penetration of this technology—the ability to do cross-border transactions on a level that has never been done in the history of humanity before.

*"Consider what we've been talking about: financial transactions, banking, payments. It's a fancy credit card. It's Paypal, basically. It's a global Paypal. But it's not. It's something completely, radically different."*

Today, there are 3 billion people with no banking facilities whatsoever. Three billion more people—"underbanked," as we call them—without any access to international credit or finance. You or I can go to a brokerage website right now and within 24 hours have a US-dollar-denominated account that can trade on the Tokyo stock exchange. That is privilege. That is a facility afforded to less than a billion people in the world. One out of seven. The other 6 billion? They barely have basic checking, if that. A lot of them live in cash- or barter-based societies. So, the question you then have to ask is what happens when a farmer in Kenya who has a Nokia 1000 text-messaging phone, and suddenly that phone is a Bloomberg terminal, a loan-origination terminal, a Western Union remittance-termination terminal, a stock market, *is* a bank—not a terminal to a bank, but a bank, on the phone? And what happens when that is afforded to the other 6 billion all over the world.

Part of the reason bitcoin is unstoppable is because there is this great need for this technology. Banks in the developing world cannot extend services to these populations. Recently, I was talking to a banker who told me, "Half our population is 100 miles from the nearest branch, upstream, on a canoe. We can't serve them." But even the remotest village in the Amazonian basin has a cell phone tower, and someone in that village has a solar panel and a Nokia 1000 text phone. There are more Nokia feature phones in the world than any other kind of electronic device. It is the most massively produced device humanity has ever produced. Almost 5 billion people have access to cell phones. Almost 3 billion people have access to cell phones and do not have access to safe drinking water. Think about that. Cell phones are more widespread than water on our planet. What happens when each and every one of those is a banker. For me, the vision of bitcoin is not to bank the other 6 billion; it's to unbank all of us. We can do it. Banking is an app.

*"For me, the vision of bitcoin is not to bank the other 6 billion; it's to unbank all of us."*

# Interstitial Innovation

That's just the beginning. The really interesting things in bitcoin happen in what I call "interstitial innovation"—the innovation in the gaps, the places where today's systems cannot go. Technologies have an interesting effect where they suddenly change basic assumptions. Some of the most powerful things that happen on the internet happen not just because of connectivity, but because of the marginal cost of transmitting information over distance. Before the internet, moving information from point A to point B cost a lot of money. The internet drove that cost almost to zero. The result was that millions of applications that could not happen on the previous cost basis, even if we could imagine them, suddenly became possible. Why on earth would you stream music instead of buy it and store it locally? Because it costs nothing. Once it costs nothing and you can stream music, then you suddenly realize that ownership is kind of overrated. If an entire generation realizes that, then intellectual property is kind of overrated. Bye-bye, recording industry. These effects happen because the technology changes the fundamental costs of doing things.

Let's think about what happens when bitcoin changes the fundamental cost of transacting—transacting across distance, transmitting value, recording information, and recording information in an immutable way. What happens when, for the first time ever, there is a system that can evaluate rules without human intervention and be trusted without having to put trust in any single human? In bitcoin, we call this the removal of counterparty risk. If I create a transaction and I sign it, everyone on the bitcoin network can validate that transaction independently. They don't have to ask anyone. They can go through the blockchain on their own machine, which they know is correct and true because they have been tracking it and building it based on proof of work. They can check that transaction, 350 bytes, and they can validate that transaction without asking anybody else. A self-verifying system, a system of rules that exists independent of human actors, that exists based on this network topology.

*"What happens when, for the first time ever, there is a system that can evaluate rules without human intervention and be trusted without having to put trust in any single human? In bitcoin, we call this the removal of counterparty risk."*

What does that mean? What does it do to commerce, to transactions? We can understand what it does to banking. We can understand that Western Union is going down hard this decade. You charge 30 percent on the poorest people in the world, you deserve to go down by disruptive technology. Last year, the CEO of Western Union said, "In the medium term, we are not worried about bitcoin." I want that framed on my wall. It's one of those phrases, like the boss of Kodak saying things like that when Nokia took away their lunch. Kodak was the largest camera company in the world until a company that wasn't in the camera business shipped a billion cameras in one year and destroyed their industry. They never saw it coming. Nokia, by the way, is the world's largest manufacturer of cameras, by far. That's going to happen to Western Union.

That's the easy stuff. What happens when you are able to do this validation of rules without a third party? It changes several fundamental societal institutions that we have today. It changes what's called the *Coase coefficient*, which is the overhead created by organization. If we want to do something as a team, two people can do more than what one person can do. Three people can achieve even more. But there's a limit to that. Once you get too big, the communication overhead between participants in the group is greater than the marginal increase in efficiency. So, adding more people makes it worse, because the group is getting bigger too fast. Bitcoin changes that, because it now reduces the coefficient of organizing on a transactional, on a commercial, on an independent-validation basis, on an extremely large scale. We can now get about a million people, about 5,000 machines, to agree on the state of a ledger every ten minutes at extremely low cost. That has never happened before. It opens the door for things that we can't even imagine. Bitcoin is radically discontinuous from the past.

Let's take one simple example: personhood. Personhood is required for financial ownership. In order to own money, in order to control funds, in order to have a bank account, to receive a bill, to pay someone, you must be a person. Everywhere in the world in every payment and financial network that exists, people own money. They may own it in the form of corporations, but that's just people grouping together. They may use proxies, agents, things like that, but that's just people working together. Bitcoin does not require personhood. A software agent can own money. A piece of software can be autonomously controlling money without any human intervention. This is completely unheard of in the history of man. We have never seen what happens next.

Here's a little thought experiment: Let's take three radically disruptive technologies and mash them together.  Bitcoin. Uber. Self-driving cars. What happens when you mash the three together? The self-owning car. A car that pays for its Toyota lease, its insurance, and its gas, by giving people rides. A car that is not owned by a corporation. A car that *is* a corporation. A car that is a shareholder and owner of its own corporation. A car that exists as an autonomous financial entity with no human ownership.  This has never happened before, and that's just the beginning. *Audience member gasps: "Oh shit!"*

> *"Let's take three radically disruptive technologies and mash them together. Bitcoin. Uber. Self-driving cars. What happens when you mash the three together? The self-owning car."*

I can guarantee you that one of the first distributed autonomous corporations is going to be a fully autonomous, artificial-intelligence-based ransomware virus that will go out and rob people online of their bitcoin, and use that money to evolve itself to pay for better programming, to buy hosting, and to spread. That's one vision of the future. Another vision of the future is a digital autonomous charity. Imagine a system that takes donations from people, and using those donations it monitors social media like Twitter and Facebook. When a certain threshold is reached and it sees 100,000 people talking about a natural disaster, like a typhoon in the Philippines, it can marshal the donations and automatically fund aid in that area, without a board of directors, without shareholders. One hundred percent of donations goes directly to charitable causes. Anyone can see the rules by which that autonomous altruistic charity works. We are beginning to approach things we have never seen before. This is not just a currency.

Now, let's look at how the bitcoin community is addressing this incredible potential with their design choices and metaphors. Oh boy, it's a mess.

# ATM Experience

Let's take a simple example. How many of you had an experience with a bitcoin ATM—or BTM, as it's known? How was that experience? Who enjoyed it?

Nobody, that's about right. What is an ATM? ATMs have been around for 25 years now. What purpose does an ATM serve? What is its goal? *Audience member: "It's a cash dispensary."* Okay. When you interact as a person with an ATM: you have a pre-existing relationship with the bank or financial institution, you have a pre-existing balance, your primary objective is to get in, get cash, get out. Twenty seconds is too long. Three clicks is too long. The most incredible innovation in ATMs in the last 25 years has been Fast Cash. That's it. They haven't really changed much. You press a button. Now, I can get cash in one click. Wow—15 seconds, in and out. Why is this important? Because one of the primary uses of ATMs is that at 1:00 in the afternoon, 100 people line up in front of four or five ATMs in the center of town and all try to take out 20 dollars to buy lunch. You see this all around the world.

What is the purpose of an ATM? For a bank, the purpose of an ATM is reducing the overhead of having a human, and reducing the interaction to the shortest possible time for someone who has a pre-existing relationship with that bank. What does that have in common with the bitcoin ATM? Absolutely nothing.

# Bitcoin ATM Experience

Now let's look at the experience of a bitcoin ATM. The average user of a bitcoin ATM is someone who has never seen bitcoin before. It is a person who doesn't understand what bitcoin is, and the ATM is their first introduction to this currency. It's a person who does not have a pre-existing relationship with anyone in the bitcoin space. It is a person who does not currently have a wallet, because they didn't know they needed one. They don't know what a wallet is, they certainly don't know it's actually a keychain. They walk up to this machine, and this machine has been designed by engineers to simulate the experience of an ATM, even though the experience shares absolutely nothing with the use case we're putting it to.

So, you walk up and the ATM tries to give you bitcoin in as few clicks as possible with a minimum amount of interaction. Is that a way to build brand loyalty? Is that a way to build user experience? Is that a way to introduce new users? I mean, it just throws it at you. You're not ready for that. *Please open your phone and display your QR code.* You're like, "What? What's a QR code? . . . Hang on, let me go to Google Play and search for 'QR code.' There's an app that scans them, . . . maybe I should use that one. Shouldn't use that one. Maybe I should use a bitcoin wallet. Oh, there are 26 of them. Which one's the best? I don't know. I'll use Circle. . . . Oh, that requires a pre-existing relationship, whoops. I'll use Coinbase. . . . Oh, that requires a pre-existing relationship, oops. . . ."

Finally, I've got my wallet and I display the QR code, put some money in, and I've got the bitcoin. What am I going to do with it? I have all these questions. Who takes bitcoin? Where can I spend this? How do I send it? How do I secure it? Will it get lost if I lose my phone? I have no clue. Why? Because this bloody infernal machine didn't tell me anything. It just threw the bitcoin at me, and in 15 seconds it's off to the next customer.

If I was designing a bitcoin ATM, first of all, I'd put it in bodegas. Secondly, it wouldn't have a lick of English on it; it would be all Spanish because I'm going to really push the remittance model. Thirdly, the first function on the ATM would be *Send Money to Mexico City*. That's it. Because I want people to use the bitcoin for something. Fourth, I'd have a big button on the front that says *Talk to a Human*. I've got an internet-connected device with a forward-facing camera and a tablet screen, and I'm not using it to do video customer service, are you kidding me? Boom: Skype. A person. "What the hell is bitcoin? Where do I spend it?" "Oh, sir, I see that you're in the bodega on 25th Avenue. There are three stores that take bitcoin in your area. Let me show you a brief introductory video. Gather all the children in the store and we can all dance to a little bitcoin song. Let's watch another video." I don't want to interact for 15 seconds. I want to interact for two hours and get all of my friends to sit in front of the machine and watch the little bitcoin videos and learn about bitcoin. It's got pretty colors, and it tells me where I can spend it. It gives me suggestions on wallets. It can send them directly to my phone. It's building loyalty, brand, and experience. That's not a 15-second interaction. This is the first experience that many people will have with bitcoin. You have the opportunity to make this a deep, meaningful, educational experience. But you don't.

## Kids Use Bitcoin

Here's another little clue: kids are using bitcoin. On average around the world, the earliest age at which you can open a bank account is 16 years old. By the time that 16-year-old goes to the bank, I want them to have at least six years of active bitcoin use in their experience. Because then, when they face their first banker, they're going to be, "Three to five days?! Business days?! What the hell is a business day? What do you *mean* you close at 5:00? I barely get off of work at 5:00. What do you mean I have to pay for you to store my money. This is ridiculous. Have you people even heard of bitcoin?!"

*"For many young people, bitcoin will be their first economic experience. By the time they get to a bank, they will be done with banking in advance."*

That's the experience I want. Guess what? Ten-year-olds are opening bitcoin accounts. You know why? They can go download the app on the internet, and they can be in control of money for the first time. So, you need to have the birds-and-bees discussion, but you also need to have the private-keys discussion. This is a huge generational divide. For many young people, bitcoin will be their first economic experience. By the time they get to a bank, they will be done with banking in advance. That's a huge advantage.

# Brand New Tech, Same Old Terms

So, how do you appeal to a completely new demographic? Part of the trick is not trying to be a bank. Do not try to do anything related to traditional banking. All that does is pollute their mind. You want new users to have a brand new experience with bitcoin that is unlike any banking they will ever see. You don't want it to look like a checking account. God forbid you use the word "checking." Open any one of the exchanges right now—Circle, Coinbase. What is the name of your account on Coinbase? It is a checking account, and it has a balance, and it shows you a statement. Who did they hire for this design? What does the word "checking" mean? It means an account on which you can write checks. I know this is America and we're 25 years behind on fintech. The rest of the world doesn't do checks, I guarantee you. What is a check? A check is the device by which a grandma can make 20 people in line behind her in the supermarket simultaneously groan. I use it to pay my rent every month. I don't know why. I can't do it any other way. It's insane that I'm signing a piece of paper and sending it through the postal system in 2015. So that my landlord can walk it through the bank and deposit it. So that it might clear three to five business days later, after they've charged him five dollars to own his own money.

We don't really need a hard sell to make bitcoin win on the banks. All you need in order for bitcoin to win against banks is for a person to use bitcoin for a week, and then the bank will take care of the rest. They'll freeze their account, they'll tell them they're closed, they'll hold it for three to five business days. They just sold bitcoin. Banks will sell it for you every single time.

# The Joys of International Wire Transfer

I was invited to do a talk at the Bundesbank, the German Federal Bank. They were paying me for this speaking engagement, but they didn't know how to do bitcoin, which is a real problem because I usually get paid in bitcoin. So, we agreed to do a wire transfer. It took 16 days. First, they asked for my account number. Then, the next day they said they needed the SWIFT number. By that time, my bank was closed, so I couldn't get the SWIFT number. The next morning, I got the SWIFT number and I sent it to the Germans. By that time, their bank was closed. The next morning, they used the SWIFT number and discovered it was the wrong SWIFT number. It was the SWIFT number for US dollars, not for foreign currency. So, they sent me an email, but by that time my bank was closed. The next day, I got the other SWIFT number and I sent it to the Germans, but by that time their bank was closed. They sent me the wire. My bank took one look at this wire and said, "Bundesbank. Never heard of them. Sounds dodgy. Let's freeze this for 14 days, just in case it bounces." This is the third largest central bank in the world. This is the German Federal Bank. They do not bounce checks. 14 days later—and this is the great part —they said, "Money held. Money released." They released 80 dollars of the total amount, which was a four-figure amount. 80 dollars. Why 80? What the hell is that? What am I going to do with that? Just hold all of it. Are you teasing me? This makes no sense.

# The Problem with Traditional Banking Metaphors

This is what we're addressing with bitcoin. If you are introducing a new product in this market and you are a designer, which parts of this design metaphor do you want to re-use in your product? According to the bitcoin marketplace, all of them, so that you can persuade people that this is just like your bank. It doesn't have any of the good parts of a bank—like the ability to easily reverse transactions, to get a refund if you lose your private key. It doesn't have any of those. It also doesn't have any of the bad parts of banks, but we don't pay attention to that. So, we've created expectations that are entirely misleading.

*"Bitcoin desperately needs design. It has been created by engineers and it is absolutely inscrutable."*

# Innovation, Design, and Adoption

Bitcoin desperately needs design. It has been created by engineers and it is absolutely inscrutable. But I have hope because we've done this before. I got on the internet in 1989, and at the time it was illegal to do commercial activities on the internet. It was owned by the National Science Foundation, and it was only for academics (or, let's say, 15-year-olds who happen to find the password to an academic system). At the time, DNS was still in its infancy. Most systems didn't really have DNS names assigned yet. It wasn't very well structured. A lot of the most interesting things you could only find via IP address. I walked around with a list of IP addresses in my wallet, so I had access to these things. In order to use it, it required UNIX command-line skills.

There was absolutely no way that was going to get used by my mom. My mom called me and told me her stereo was broken, and I tried to figure out why. She said, "It's displaying an error message. It's blinking at me '0:00.'" It took me a few minutes to figure out that she had pulled the plug and the clock had reset. So, the clock was waiting to be set again and was blinking "0:00." That's the person who I wanted to use the internet so we could talk, but that wasn't going to happen. It took almost exactly 20 years from the day I sent my first email to the day my mom sent her first email. In order to do so, a lot of things had to happen. Most importantly, the iPad. She was able to do it with a swipe of a finger, and that was the only thing that made it possible. There was no way *that* internet in 1989 could be used by the mainstream.

## UX and Society

There's this fantastic outtake from a morning TV show in 1994 in which the journalists are in a huddle just before the show. They are discussing their upcoming internet story, and they're trying to get their information right. One journalist is asking the other journalists, "So, wait, the internet is the thing with the 'at' sign?" "No, no, that's email. The internet is the thing with the 'www,' with the dots and the slashes." "I thought that was the email." "No, that's the internet." "But isn't that the web?" So there's this circular discussion. A system designed by engineers. Inscrutable. Two things happened. One, we made the technology much easier to understand, much better, more polished. Another important thing happened: society moved. Today, the average person knows exactly the difference between an @ sign and a www, even though it's a horrible design. Society learned the language of the internet because it was valuable enough to learn the language of the internet.

*"Society learned the language of the internet because it was valuable enough to learn the language of the internet."*

While we made the internet easier, society caught up and also understood the really inscrutable parts of the internet. The same thing is happening with bitcoin. I go to mainstream conferences where they have never heard of bitcoin before and I say, "Listen, don't worry. Someone in your life can explain bitcoin to you. When they're done cleaning their room, ask them to teach you bitcoin." Their 10-year-old will understand it. I've met kids that use web-based interfaces to create altcoins of their own.

One of the interesting questions I get often is "How many coins and currencies will there be?" The answer to that is exactly equivalent to "How many bloggers will there be on the internet?" All of us. All of them. Not hundreds of coins; thousands, tens of thousands of coins. When a 6-year-old can create a coin called Joeycoin to launch in his school as a popularity contest, the fact that that coin is also global, unforgeable, scalable, and can be used internationally doesn't matter to Joey, as long as his five friends really like to use Joeycoin. Unfortunately, a competitor, Mariacoin, is launched on the scene, and an old-fashioned currency war starts. This is going to happen. Part of the reason we know this is because children create currency. You leave children in a kindergarten by themselves, and they will invent currency—rubber bands, Pokémon cards, little cubes. They will start hoarding, trading, exchanging for favors, and then eventually getting into a fight over their imaginary currency that they just invented. This is a human experience.

*We* just invented the world's most awesome currency. Your job now is to create the right design metaphors to make it work for everybody else.

Thank you.

# Money as a Content Type

*Bitcoin South Conference; Queenstown, New Zealand; November 2014*

Video Link: https://www.youtube.com/watch?v=6vFgBGdmDgs

Good morning, everyone. What I want to talk about today is a new topic I've been working on: money as a content type. Bitcoin has introduced a fundamental transformation in how money is going to be viewed in the future by making money completely independent of the underlying transport medium and turning it into a stand-alone content type.

What do I mean by that? A bitcoin transaction is a signed data structure that can be executed anywhere in the world. A lot of people think that a bitcoin transaction has to be transmitted on the bitcoin network. That's not true. A bitcoin transaction has to reach the miners and be included in a block, but it doesn't need to be transmitted over the bitcoin network. There's nothing special about the bitcoin network. It just forwards transactions and blocks. A transaction can be transmitted over any form of communication medium.

One of the magic things about bitcoin is that the transaction doesn't incorporate security mechanisms itself. The security is in the proof of work provided by the miners, and the digital signature on the transaction is put there by end users with keys that they store. There's nothing sensitive or secret in the bitcoin transaction. Let me explain what I mean by that.

## Credit Cards: Insecure by Design

If I go to a merchant today using a point-of-sale system and a credit card, what I am transmitting to the merchant (through a long series of intermediaries) is the credit card number, expiry date, and CCV2 code on the back of the card. I'm actually transmitting the secret keys. I'm transmitting the access codes to my account. That information is sensitive. If that information is captured, my account can be compromised. I can be charged again and again, either by the merchant or one of the intermediaries, or any hacker who has taken this information from any of the intermediaries. My credit card information needs to be very carefully protected.

From the moment the credit card comes out of my pocket until the money is in the merchant's account, it is transported across the network in a series of virtual armored cars. There's encryption from the point of sale to the merchant's back end. From the merchant's back end, encryption through to Visa for batch processing. From Visa, encryption through to the originating bank and to the destination bank, encrypting this token at every step of the way because it is the secret key.

If that encryption fails at any point in the chain, the security of my credit card is compromised.

That credit card is also stored at many of the points of transit. It's stored for historical purposes. Which is a terrible idea because that creates a centralized treasure trove, a stash for hackers to attack. We've seen this happen again and again. In the US, Target and Home Depot, two very large retailers, have had incidents where they've had 50 to 60 million credit cards stolen. JPMorgan Chase had 75 million accounts compromised recently. All of these things are not happening because these companies are delinquent in protecting credit cards.

> *"There are really two types of companies out there: those that have failed to take the necessary action to secure the credit cards that you entrusted them with; and those that will soon fail to take the necessary security action to protect the credit cards you've entrusted them with... Credit cards are broken by design because the token itself is the secret key. If you transmit that token, you expose your entire account to risk."*

There are really two types of companies out there: those that have failed to take the necessary action to secure the credit cards that you entrusted them with; and those that will soon fail to take the necessary security action to protect the credit cards you've entrusted them with. You've either been hacked or you will be hacked— those are the two categories. Nobody's immune to this. No one can invent a way to protect millions of secure access tokens from motivated attackers. It's impossible to do. We don't know how to do it. There is no information security trick that can protect for all possible types of attacks. Credit cards are broken by design because the token itself is the secret key. If you transmit that token, you expose your entire account to risk.

# Bitcoin Transactions: Secure by Design

Bitcoin is fundamentally different. What I'm transmitting is not the key, but simply a signed message. It is an authorization. That authorization has two external references: (1) to where the money's coming from by referencing an unspent output on the blockchain, and (2) a reference to where I want to send the money — by creating a new encumbrance, a new limitation on who can spend the money, usually a public key or bitcoin address. That transaction contains no sensitive data. If you steal the information in the transaction, all you know is which address the money came from, which address the money's going to, and how much. That's it. The signature reveals nothing. The addresses reveal nothing. There are no identifiers. You could take the transaction and print it out. You could post it on a billboard. You could shout it from the rooftop. A bitcoin transaction can be transmitted over completely unsecured Wi-Fi. By smoke signal. By light signal. With carrier pigeons. It doesn't matter. Nothing in that message can be compromised.

> *"A bitcoin transaction can be transmitted over completely unsecured Wi-Fi. By smoke signal. By light signal. With carrier pigeons. It doesn't matter. Nothing in that message can be compromised."*

## Money as a Content Type

Most people don't realize what it means to convert money into a content type. We've taken the transaction, which is just 250 bytes, and we've separated it from the transport medium, so it doesn't depend on any underlying security. We've made it stand alone so that it can be independently verified by any node that has a full copy of the blockchain. Independently verified as spendable, authentic, and properly signed by *any* system that has a full copy of the blockchain—in fact, even by systems that only have a partial copy of the blockchain. That transaction can be verified in seconds. All it has to do is reach one node in the network that can talk to miners. That's it. Once it's injected into the bitcoin network and once it propagates, you can be almost certain that the transaction will be included eventually and will become valid. If I look at any transaction, I can calculate if it has sufficient fees, and then I can make certain assumptions about how miners are going to treat that transaction because I know the rules by which they operate on a consensus network. I know that once the transaction is propagated enough, it will appear in a block near you, soon.

## Stopping Bitcoin Transactions Is Impossible

There's nothing magical in a bitcoin transaction. Let's think about this for a second. How can you encode 250 bytes and transmit them across the network?

Someone recently asked me, and I get this question a lot, "Can't tyrannical governments block or ban the transmission of bitcoin transactions?" The answer is *no*, but I don't think people quite understand *why* the answer is no. I'll give you a couple of theoretical examples to show what I mean.

## Transmitting Bitcoin Transactions via Skype as Smileys

My first ridiculous example is the encoding of bitcoin transactions as emoticons or smileys in Skype. Skype has a 128-character emoji alphabet which allows you to send various frowny faces, smiley faces, thumbs up, thumbs down, sunny days, beating hearts, birthday cakes—you know, all of those kinds of things. Now, let's look at that from an information-content perspective. That's a character set, right? If I'm a computer scientist, I'm going to look at that and say, okay, I now have an encoding scheme. This would allow me to send a 250-byte transaction in about 500 characters. 500 smileys. A bitcoin transaction in smileys.

I can literally mathematically write a little script, it's two lines of Python probably. If you're really efficient, it's probably one line. No libraries needed. In the script, I can take the hexadecimal representation of a bitcoin transaction and encode it in emoticons. I can then copy that into a Skype window anywhere in the world. As long as the recipient who receives that string of smileys types it into a decoder script and then simply injects it into the bitcoin network, that transaction will go through. The recipient could be a robot. The recipient could be an automated listening station that is designed to decode smileys into transactions and transmit them onto the bitcoin network.

Now, explain to me how anyone can make that stop, other than by shutting down Skype. If they shut down Skype, I'll use Facebook. If they shut down Facebook, I'll use Craigslist. If they shut down Craigslist, I'll put my transaction in a TripAdvisor review. If they shut down TripAdvisor, I'll post it as a comment in the history of a Wikipedia article. If they shut that down, I'll post it as the background of a JPEG image in my holiday snapshots.

> *"Money is now completely disconnected information content."*

Money is now completely disconnected information content. There is absolutely nothing you can do to stop information from traveling from anywhere in the world to anywhere in the world when you have an abundance of fully interconnected multimedia communication mechanisms as we do today.

# Transmitting Bitcoin Transactions via Shortwave Radio

Let's say we didn't have the internet. I came up with an even more ridiculous harebrained scheme, which is the transmission of bitcoin transactions over shortwave, frequency-hopping, burst radio. This is if you want to go completely guerrilla-style.

During the Second World War, in occupied France, the Allies dropped thousands of shortwave radios — complete kits with little parachutes — from airplanes, so that Partisans on the ground could hide these in barns, in tree hollows, in abandoned buildings, under bridges, and use them to communicate with various Allied command centers around Europe, from right under the nose of the occupying Nazi force. One of the things about shortwave radio is that not only do you have enormous range, but you can also, in certain frequencies, bounce off the stratosphere. At the time, they used this for voice communication or coded numbers communication, Morse code and various one-time pad encryption schemes.

Today, I can get a kit that allows me to connect a very simplistic shortwave radio transmitter to my laptop via USB. Now all I need is an antenna. The nice thing about that is that with shortwave radio, an antenna consists of a sufficiently long piece of metal — a railway line, a clothesline, a broken-down electricity line, a fence line, a razor-wire fence. Which, I've noticed here in New Zealand you have lots of. It's right around those fuzzy white things that are everywhere — the sheep.

Now, the transmission of a bitcoin transaction involves plugging in a laptop, attaching it to a fence post, pressing "enter," and transmitting a burst transaction for 25 seconds. As long as there's a receiving station somewhere within the surrounding thousand miles that is connected to the bitcoin network — and you can hide the receiving station anywhere you want, it's a passive listener, it can't be triangulated — that listening device can inject the transaction into the network. If I'm the guerrilla and I want to buy something, I construct the transaction offline, and when I'm ready, run out into the middle of the field, clamp my transmitter onto a clothesline, press "enter," transmit for 25 seconds, pack up my gear, and disappear into the forest. How the hell do you stop that? You don't. That's the simple answer, you don't. But that's just the beginning.

# Separating the Medium and the Message

Once you realize that money has become a content type, that transactions have been disconnected from the medium, some really important secondary characteristics emerge. You see, the medium is the message, as someone famous once said. The primary reason the medium is the message is because the medium constrains, transforms, and in many cases, distorts the message.

When your medium is TV, your message is 18 minutes long, interrupted by advertising slots. That is your message; there is no other format you can fit there. So, you make a message that fits that medium. And you start assigning the value of your message based on the mistaken assumption that it is equivalent to the cost of production. TV, for example, imposes a certain cost to producing video. People who are in that business make the mistaken assumption that the cost of producing TV is the same as the value of that show. The more you spend on it, the more valuable it is.

You can imagine their horror when something like YouTube comes along and drops the cost of production to zero. What do you think is the immediate assumption that people make in that industry? If the cost is zero, then the content is worthless. That is a fundamental misunderstanding of what happens when you separate the content from the medium. By separating the message from the medium, your perception of value shifts from the cost of production to the value it has to the consumer when they consume it.

> *"When the cost of printing is astronomical and the means of printing are available only to a select few, the only thing you print is Gutenberg Bibles."*

Let me give you an even older example. When the cost of printing is astronomical and the means of printing are available only to a select few, the only thing you print is Gutenberg Bibles. The medium defines the range of expression of the message, and constrains it only to the most grandiose and important messages that society has. It limits the range of expression by imposing enormous costs of production.

What do you think Gutenberg would have thought of Twitter, which takes the cost of production to zero, makes it available universally, ubiquitously, and for free. You go from printing the Gutenberg Bible to responding to a tweet with one of my favorite expressions, the three-character opinion "SMH" — which means "shaking my head." When "Professor Bitcorn" says, "Bitcoin is going to zero," I can express my entire range of opinion and thoughtful analysis as *shakes head with facepalm*. Three characters, and I have expressed my opinion to the world. If you look at that from an objective perspective, surely that message is worthless. When you make the mistaken assumption that if the cost of production is zero, and the message appears trivial on its face, then the entire combination of medium plus message must be worthless, must be trivial, must have no value — that's a mistake that people have made at every turn in history.

When Twitter first came out, people assumed it would only be used for the trivial. And yet, a year ago I was watching *CNN International* covering the Egyptian revolution, and they were live-streaming tweets from Egyptian revolutionaries on the streets of Cairo, giving live reports about what is happening minute-by-minute. CNN anchors are doing nothing. They're pointing at the screen and saying, "Look, we have another tweet. And here's another tweet from someone we don't know. Here's another tweet." They've been reduced to the role of a TV show model saying, "And this wonderful refrigerator will be yours if you win the prize behind door number one." I find it extremely gratifying to watch one of these talking heads, like Anderson Cooper, basically reduced to reading tweets off a screen.

Because they mocked it. They made the mistaken assumption that if the cost of production is zero, the value of the message is zero. They confused the medium for the message. They made the mistaken assumption that their control over the medium was the source of quality. And long after quality disappeared, they clung to control and thought that control was the only way to achieve quality, and if you removed control, you removed quality. That is stinky, unabashed elitism at its absolute worst. It assumes that the gatekeepers are the source of quality, when all they are is gatekeepers. They assume that the fact that they have the expensive medium means that the message is worth listening to.

> *"They made the mistaken assumption that if the cost of production is zero, the value of the message is zero. They confused the medium for the message. They made the mistaken assumption that their control over the medium was the source of quality. And long after quality disappeared, they clung to control..."*

The moment you tear that message away from the medium and you open it up to an entire range of expression, yes, it will express the most trivial messages of your culture, including "SMH." But it will also express the most interesting messages of your culture, eventually.

Today in US schools, children read *The Federalist Papers*, which is a collection of public essays written in the 18th century by some of the founding fathers debating the meaning of democracy for the new republic. In 100 years, people will be reading *The Federalist Tweets of the Cairo Revolution*. That's not an insane idea. That is the path of human civilization. We've seen this happen again and again.

Now, they mock Twitter as trivial because they don't understand the distinction between message and medium. TV was once mocked as a trivial pastime because it obscured the art of cinematography. Cinematography was a trivial pastime because it cheapened and vulgarized the art of the theater. The theater was a vulgar and cheap pastime of Victorians because it trivialized the great dramatic plays of the Romans and the Ancient Greeks. You keep going down this path and you'll eventually arrive at Aristotle saying that philosophy is dead because nowadays the kids all want to watch dramatic presentations instead of reading their philosophy books. He probably complained about their long hair, too. Every generation mistakes the medium for value and considers the next iteration of the medium—that widens access, that opens availability, that broadens the range of expression—they consider that medium trivial, vulgar, cheapening the message.

> *"Every generation mistakes the medium for value and considers the next iteration of the medium —that widens access, that opens availability, that broadens the range of expression—they consider that medium trivial, vulgar, cheapening the message."*

What they don't understand is when you cheapen the medium, you release the message and you elevate it. You are able now to express a broad range of messages. Yes, the first ones will be trivial. The reason they'll be trivial is because the previous medium didn't allow for that expression. It didn't have within it the ability to have that expression. Yes, you will have the "SMH." You'll also have live tweets from the Cairo revolution. By the time they figure that out, the new medium *is* the quality message. Then, we can turn around and call the next one vulgar and cheap.

# Money Is the Message, Now Freed from the Medium

Money is a content type, and we just wrenched it free from the medium. The medium has been a series of interconnected networks that segregate money by size and recipient. We have payment networks for small money. We have payment networks for large money. We have payment networks for fast money. We have payment networks for slow money. Payment networks for businesses to pay businesses. Payment networks for governments to pay governments. Payment networks for consumers to pay businesses. Payment networks for consumers to pay consumers. Oh wait, we don't really have those. We don't have payment networks for consumers to pay consumers. We don't have payment networks to do small payments because the traditional medium does not allow that range of expression.

> *"Money is a content type, and we just wrenched it free from the medium."*

I cannot send you 20 cents across the world, from one individual to another individual, because the medium constrains the message. The cost of production does not allow me to express that range of transactional expression. But now we have separated the message from the medium. We have created money as a content type. That money is now able, at near zero production cost, to express the entire range of transactional expression—from the tiny to the enormous, from consumer to consumer, from government to government.

What happens next? The gatekeepers tell you that this network is not serious. The gatekeepers confuse their payment-network cost for the value of their service. The gatekeepers of the old payment networks will tell you that this new form of payment is vulgar and cheap. It is something that is only used for trivialities. All of the very serious people will remain on the solid, quality payment networks of the past. Because if they can control and restrict the range of expression, they think that means it's quality. It's not. It's just an inflated cost of production. It's bare naked elitism at its worst. They cling to the medium and fail to see that now the message can be transported over any medium at zero cost, instantaneously.

What is the first use of this new model? What is the first use of this new messaging medium? Now we can send trivial payments. I get tips on Twitter. That's a demonstration I can make that clearly shows people the difference. I can do something I could not do before. But to most people, that's trivial. To most people, the fact that I'm showing them the bottom of the range of expression simply reinforces the idea that this is a cheap and vulgar medium. What they fail to grasp is that this medium is not just for the trivial; it spans the entire range of transactional expression from the trivial to the enormous.

> *"The blockchain can encompass the entire range*
> *of transactional expression, from the 10-cent*
> *tweet to the $100 billion debt settlement."*

One day, a country will pay its oil bill on the blockchain. One day, you might buy a multinational company on the blockchain. One day, you might sell an aircraft carrier, hopefully for scrap metal, on the blockchain. The blockchain can encompass the entire range, from the 10-cent tweet to the $100 billion debt settlement. We just haven't noticed yet. It can do so without any constraint imposed by the underlying medium. This isn't just a matter of the fact that the transaction as a content type can be transported over Skype smileys. That's simply a symptom of the fact that we have released all of the constraints of the underlying transport medium. We have made content king.

# Grand Arc of Technology

When content begins as the domain of exclusivity, elitism, and limited access, it is used by grandmasters to create masterpieces. The Gutenberg Bible. The first photographs. The landing on the moon, televised for the first time. The great movies of the past. Masterpieces made by grandmasters.

Then the medium changes because the technology becomes more available. People start using it for a broader range of expression, but the gatekeepers still cling to the old ideas. They still try to do the grandiose with their medium. They print hardback, heavy, leather-bound books—*Principia Mathematica*. Then the medium opens up again and things become softcover, and photographs become available to the everyday person in 24 exposures. The gatekeepers of the past still cling to the past, but now they can't really pretend that it's grandiose, so they just do grandstanding. They say, "There's a certain *je ne sais quoi* to film." "There's a certain quality to vinyl that CDs will never capture." "A TV anchor really has authority. Don't you remember Walter Cronkite?" "A newspaper is the source of authoritative opinion, and it really is worth the paper it's printed on." Grandstanding. The grandiosity is gone. The quality is gone. Now, it's just a matter of clinging to the control and pretending that control is still quality.

Finally, in this grand arc of technology, the technology reaches the final stage. In that final stage, the only people who still believe it's grand are grandparents. In the grand arc of technology, what started out as a masterpiece is now only consumed by those in the last stages of their lives. The first checks written out were used by royalty to fund great ventures like the East India Company to open the spice roads and trade routes to the East. In those days, only royals had checkbooks. Today, if you go into a supermarket and the grandmother, bless her heart, in front of you in the line opens up her purse and pulls out the checkbook, 15 people in line are going to groan audibly as they realize it's going to take 15 minutes to write out that transaction. There's nothing left of the grandiosity of funding the East India Company when you're buying beans and toast with a checkbook in a supermarket. It's the final stage.

The only people watching *Fox News* now are grandparents, because we all get our news on the internet. What was once trivial is now our source of authoritative news and information. You can't explain that to the old guard. We read our books electronically. Some people say, "There's something about the feel of paper." Yes. It's too heavy to carry 20 books in your bag, and I read 20 books in four or five weeks, so I need to carry that many. There's nothing about the feel of paper; that's clinging to the past.

> *"As we move into this world where money is a content type, the gatekeepers of the old payment systems will cling to the illusion that traditional banking is quality. That the gatekeepers are the quality. But that's not where the quality is."*

As we move into this world where money is a content type, the gatekeepers of the old payment systems will cling to the illusion that traditional banking is quality. That the gatekeepers are the quality. That the quality is inherent in the gatekeeping —in the control, in the censorship, in the limitations. But that's not where the quality is. We're moving on and opening up the range of expression that is possible with money to unimaginable levels, to things that have never happened before. They'll still cling to their ideas of grandiosity: the great old banks with the vaulted ceilings and the chromed vaults that are empty, where you can get guided tours on Sundays, to look at what banks used to be like. You can go into cities around the world and the great vaults of the great old banks are now bars where you can get a cocktail in the vault, because banks can't even afford to have those buildings anymore. They serve no purpose other than grandiosity. They'll still try to persuade you that through their control, they protect you from evil, from terrorists, from money launderers. All they're doing is protecting their own incumbency from competition.

We have now separated the message from the medium. Money is now a content type, and we're never going back.

Thank you.

*Note from Andreas to the reader: In this talk I foolishly attempted to improvise math in my head while delivering the talk. I am not very good at math. Turns out I am even worse at improv-math. None of my bad math changes the point I was making, but it's been edited out for accuracy and to protect my ego. Ssssh! Don't tell anyone I suck at improv-math.*

# Elements of Trust: Unleashing Creativity

*Blockchain Meetup; Berlin, Germany; March 2016*

Video Link: https://www.youtube.com/watch?v=uLpSM3HWU6U

Today, I'm going to talk about the chemistry of money, specifically the chemistry of bitcoin. This is one of the aspects of bitcoin that makes it so exciting and so interesting. It's one that most of us don't even notice until we study bitcoin for a year or two. Bitcoin is a bit like an onion. You have to unwrap it. As you unwrap it, you find one more layer. I started five years ago. I am still unwrapping. I am finding more and more things that surprise me every day about bitcoin.

## The Illusion of Senders, Receivers, and Accounts

When I first encountered bitcoin, I was surprised to see that it looked like a relatively familiar banking system. I visited well-known bitcoin sites, like blockchain.info, and I could see transactions. I clicked on the transactions and I could see a sender, receiver, and account. I thought, *This is pretty familiar. Banking. Great.* Then, I decided to look at the source code and see how it worked.

As a computer scientist, I figured I'd read the source code, and I'd try to understand how the system does these things. But when I searched the source code for sender, receiver or account, I didn't find anything. Because none of those things actually exist in bitcoin. That really surprised me because when I looked at the source code, none of the things that I expected to find there were actually there. You'd expect that a banking system, as it appeared to be, had been designed to do certain things in a very specific way. Bitcoin isn't like that. It's not like that at all.

> *"When I searched the source code for sender, receiver or account, I didn't find anything. Because none of those things actually exist in bitcoin."*

How many of you have looked into the source code or understand the technical underpinnings? A few people in this room. When you dig through the code, you find there is no balance, no sender, but there is UTXO *unspent transaction outputs* and there are inputs. But those inputs don't really correspond to senders. And a transaction has outputs, which don't really correspond to receivers. Suddenly, you realize what you're looking at is almost this quantum or atomic nature of bitcoin.

# Bitcoin's Atomic Structure

In chemistry, we have elements like copper, iron, and helium. Chemistry gives you this enormous complexity of things that you can combine to make interesting things. Like people. And toasters. But when you dig into the chemistry, you realize copper isn't a thing. Copper is a pattern of protons, neutrons, and electrons. There is no copper. One proton is the same as another proton; it can just as happily be part of helium or copper, it doesn't care. There is nothing about that specific proton that makes it part of copper.

Chemistry is one layer, but underneath that is atomic physics. That layer is very simple. It has a handful of elements. This handful of just a few elements makes up all of the chemistry we know, 100+ elements in nature that all have unique and different properties, that are completely different. Some of them are liquid, some of them are metals, some of them are gases. They behave differently. Some are acidic, some are not. But none of that is their basic makeup. These are just patterns.

Bitcoin has this fundamental atomic structure, this elemental structure. The elements of bitcoin are the components of transactions and the elements of the scripting language. Those elements have nothing to do with traditional banking. There are no accounts and balances and senders and receivers. Instead, bitcoin's elements are looking for fundamental mathematical properties and cryptographic properties — such as whether a hash is equal to another hash, whether an elliptic curve signature matches another elliptic curve signature, manipulation of numbers, etc., etc. What you see on the surface — the transactions — are just constructs. They're a specific way of mashing up the elements that creates something that kind of looks like a bank. Which is great because if you're new to bitcoin and someone tells you, "Well, there is an account, a sender, and a receiver," you think, *Okay, I understand this.*

> *"What you see on the surface — the transactions — are just constructs. They're a specific way of mashing up the elements that creates something that kind of looks like a bank."*

Then you learn that you have a wallet, but your wallet doesn't have coins, it has keys, and those keys could be copied, and now you're thinking, *You're losing me. This doesn't quite match my experience.* Things get complicated because bitcoin isn't what you think it is. It's a platform. It's not a payment network. It's not a currency. It's not a banking system. It's a platform that guarantees certain trust functions. If you happen to have a platform that guarantees certain trust functions, one very useful application for that is to build a currency and a payment network, but you can build more things.

> *"Bitcoin isn't what you think it is. It's a platform. It's not a payment network. It's not a currency. It's not a banking system. It's a platform that guarantees certain trust functions."*

## Building Blocks of Lego

When I was a child, my favorite toy was Lego. The reason my favorite toy was Lego was not because of what was on the box. Because I did not build what was on the box. If the box had a red firetruck, I would build a dragon, or a hippopotamus-giraffe, something that didn't exist or some strange idea that I had. That's what I liked about it. I could take these basic building blocks, and I could build whatever I wanted.

From an abstract perspective, Lego is messy. And the thing I built didn't quite look like a firetruck or a spaceship. If someone had given me a toy that was a firetruck, like a plastic-injected, smooth-edged, completed red firetruck, it would be the perfect firetruck. But it could only ever be a firetruck, and 20 minutes after I start playing with it, I am bored. Because my smooth, rounded firetruck that is only a firetruck, is a perfect firetruck. But it could never be a hippopotamus-giraffe or a tomato or a spaceship. But Lego allows more.

## Building Blocks of Cooking

As I grew older, I started getting into cooking as a hobby. What I loved about cooking is that it is the perfect combination of art and science. If you fundamentally understand how the ingredients work, how they behave, and how the chemistry changes when they're combined or when you add a catalyst like salt or when you apply heat to them, then you can create. You can create almost anything. As long as you understand how the ingredients work, you can execute and deliver anything you want to create.

## Building Blocks of Creativity

Bitcoin encompasses that elemental nature. It doesn't give you a final result. It gives you a set of ingredients and a recipe. It gives you a set of Lego blocks and a photo on the box that looks like a red firetruck. When we present that to the world, the financial companies look at that and say, "Well, your firetruck has sharp edges and it's made of silly little blocks." In bitcoin, we take the ingredients, we put them together and we've made a banking payment system. The banks look at it and it's as if they're saying to us, "Your burger is okay but at McDonald's we can make it in 45 seconds and we can sell a billion of them. So, why do you need a chef, ingredients, a recipe, if you can just churn out a billion of them?" They're missing the point.

> *"Bitcoin encompasses that elemental nature. It doesn't give you a final result. It gives you a set of ingredients and a recipe."*

The point is not generating a billion copies of the same inferior product. The point is not getting the injection-molded plastic red truck that I am going to be bored of in 5 seconds. The point is unleashing my creativity by giving me the tools and the elements I need to build something unique.

I didn't build a burger as fast or cheap as McDonald's, and my little red firetruck isn't as smooth as the molded copy. But I can make albondigas with red tomato sauce. I can also make a hippopotamus-giraffe. You can't do that with a prefabricated toy. You can't do that in your McDonald's kitchen. I've unleashed my creativity.

## Building Blocks of Bitcoin

We're beginning to see people realize that bitcoin is a set of ingredients and you have one recipe, but you can make a different recipe. People are now trying to recombine these ingredients.

We're building crowdfunding projects by combining atomic transactions and input-versus-output sums and digital signatures. By combining these ingredients, we can create a single transaction that can be funded by multiple people, but the transaction will only be valid if the threshold funding is met. Those are the same elements I use to make a payment of a dollar to you over bitcoin's payment network, but you can recombine them differently and now you've got a crowdfunding platform.

We're building payment channels by combining 2-of-2 signatures, multisignature, with transaction time locks. This allows us to charge for video-streaming by the second. That's a whole new recipe.

We're building on top of payment channels. By taking them and adding a new ingredient, Hash Time Locked Contracts, we can connect multiple channels together. Then we've got Lightning Network, and that's a new recipe that nobody has ever seen before.

*"We're trying to unleash the creativity of an entire generation. We're building a system, on top of which a thousand applications that require trust can be built."*

The banks are saying, "Your truck has sharp corners and your burger is too expensive and took more than 45 seconds." What they're really saying is, "Your transaction fees are too high and you're too slow and you can't possibly scale." *They're missing the point.* The point is that we're not trying to sell a billion burgers at 45 seconds each; we're trying to unleash the creativity of an entire generation. We're building a system, on top of which a thousand applications that require trust can be built.

# Focus-Group Economies

When you have the ingredients, when you have these basic elements, what recipe you build is entirely up to you. Because when they build the little red firetruck, they create an entire factory that can only do little red firetrucks. I'm sure they'll tell you, "Listen, our statistics say that 95 percent of children want a little red firetruck. We have tested this with focus groups and the marketing teams. We can produce them by the millions. They only cost 3 cents. They have a very small amount of lead paint and poisonous, toxic, carcinogenic hydrocarbons, not a problem. We can do that very cheaply and very profitably." And they can only build firetrucks.

When you build a kitchen like McDonald's, you can churn out burgers every 45 seconds, but you can't make albondigas. You can't make something else. You are streamlined to do one thing and one thing only, and as long as that serves your profit line, it's okay. Because I am sure you focus-group tested it to make sure that is what everybody wanted.

That is a terrible way to build an economy. That's a terrible way to build a financial system. That's a terrible way to build a payment network.

# Banking Privilege and Surveillance

Effectively, what the banks are saying to us is, "We focus tested this. What people want is the ability, instead of swiping their Visa card, to wave it over the reader, saving almost two seconds and reducing their effort by at least four calories. I mean, we could deal with the 4 billion people who have no access to banking or clean water. We could deal with the fact that our world is a fragmented mess, where the vast majority of humanity have no access to financial services. Or, we could reduce the shopper's effort and make a swipe card into a float card.

We could face the fact that the reason more than 4 billion people are unbanked is because we require everyone to be identified on every side of every transaction, so that we can build a totalitarian surveillance system that the Stasi would be jealous of, to monitor every financial transaction from every corner of the planet. Because we have persuaded ourselves that our bourgeois sense of security will be protected, not by solving poverty, and not by reducing, perhaps, the bombing of other countries, but instead, by watching everyone all the time when they buy a burger—just in case.

We subject ourselves to this mechanism that has now streamlined itself, and like the factory that can only produce little red firetrucks, this is a system that can only deliver privileged financial services for a tiny elite sliver of the population worldwide, with totalitarian surveillance tied up in regulations of each country, with barriers on the borders not permitting international trade. A financial system where the government can apply pressure to stop you trading with WikiLeaks, because they don't like them, but you can still send donations to the Ku Klux Klan—and that's not a joke. That's exactly what happened.

They have built a system that can only do one thing: enslave us. That can only do one thing: impoverish us. That system removes freedom in the most efficient possible way to deliver profits. That system is broken, and it doesn't scale. But if that is what you're trying to do, it's the most efficient you've ever seen.

By comparison, the crazy little mishmash system that we've built with bitcoin, that's wrong and it's slow and it can't scale. It's inefficient and it's not as serious and sophisticated as the international banking system. But it delivers freedom and it allows us to unleash creativity.

Thank you.

# Scaling Bitcoin

*Bitcoin Meetup at Paralelni Polis; Prague, Czech; March 2016*

Video Link: https://www.youtube.com/watch?v=bFOFqNKKns0

## Stories of Scaling

Today, I'm going to talk about scaling. A lot of you probably have noticed that there is a very interesting debate in bitcoin today about how to scale bitcoin. That's the topic I want to address, not from a technical perspective but from a broader perspective, to try to understand what it means to scale.

## Usenet Will Destroy the Internet

Gather around and we will talk about a long time ago. It was 1989 and the internet was dial-up. Not just the connection of users to the internet; in most cases, the backbones to the internet were dial-up. Between universities, between research stations, there were a few permanent high-speed connections — 256 kilobits, 512 kilobits. But the internet was mostly dial-up. Email had not yet really started to take hold, but there was a special place on the internet called Usenet. Usenet was a system of discussion groups where you could post a message in text and other people would see it and then they would respond.

This was not instant messaging. This was *slow* messaging because, in order for Usenet to work, all of the messages had to be transmitted via dial-up systems and propagated from node to node in a system called *store and forward*. You would post a message and it would take between 24 and 48 hours to reach everyone. Then, they could respond and it would take 24 to 48 hours for you to see their response. Today, we would compare that to trying to communicate with Matt Damon on Mars, like in *The Martian* movie.

At that moment, there was a big conversation among the engineers of the internet because Usenet was getting very popular and it was getting very big. Kilobytes and then megabytes of text information needed to be transmitted. At first, it would take about 30 minutes on a dial-up connection to get all of the Usenet messages for a day. Then, as the system became more popular, more messages meant more data and more time. Soon, it was taking one hour, two hours, and three hours. And the experts predicted the end. They said, if you draw a point at where we are today and another at where we were six months ago, and connect them in a line, very soon it will take 26 hours to transmit one day's messages and then we have a problem because we only have 24.

So, what happens then? The internet will collapse! Clearly, it can't scale. It won't possibly scale.

## Alt Groups Will Destroy the Internet

At the time, there were two parts to Usenet. There was the regular part of Usenet, which contained very carefully structured groups for academic discussions, and then there was another little part of Usenet called *the alt*, the alternative groups.   The alt was optional. As a Usenet provider, you could carry alt if you wanted to but you didn't have to. The really interesting providers offered the alt groups. Of course, all of the interesting stuff was in the alt groups: some of the early amazing groups, alt.folklore.computers, alt.security, and of course, like everything else that's been driving scale on the internet, alt.sex.

These alternative groups, being optional, were the focus of this great debate. Should we carry them? Because at this point we started seeing the world's first spam.  I remember receiving the first spam. It was a message by a couple of lawyers that was posted to every Usenet group. You did not do that. That was not cool. A thousand people told them it was not cool. That was the first internet backlash.

The discussion was, do we carry alt groups? Because if we carry alt groups, the internet will surely melt down and there is no way it could ever scale. If this becomes popular, people will discuss more, and if they discuss more, we won't have enough capacity to deal with this data. This conversation lasted for more than two years. There were a few brave service providers that carried the alt groups, and they used massive hard drives—huge 5MB hard drives. Again, the main idea was, if you take the where-we-are-here and where-we're-going-up-there, we hit a wall.

> *"If we carry alt groups, the internet will surely melt down and there is no way it could ever scale."*

So, the internet couldn't scale. That was the basic beginning of the scaling issue on the internet. It couldn't scale, wouldn't scale, clearly. Many people wrote their Ph.D. theses on why it wouldn't scale.

But of course, the thing is, networks don't scale. Networks fail to scale. Some networks fail to scale gracefully for decades, and those are the ones that succeed.

*"Some networks fail to scale gracefully for
decades, and those are the ones that succeed."*

Eventually, we solved the Usenet problem. Digital connections were upgraded, more systems connected with leased lines and direct connections. Dial-up was gradually replaced by leased lines. People started investing in the infrastructure and we could comfortably carry Usenet. Then, people started using email. And the scaling problem returned.

# Email and Email Attachments Will Destroy the Internet

As email became popular, it started replacing and eclipsing the size of Usenet. Now, we had an even bigger problem because people wanted to communicate directly. Now, a message didn't take 24 hours, it took two hours to cross the internet, which meant that people started having real-time conversations—well, near real-time. Email use exploded. And again, the internet couldn't scale because if you look at where email is today and where it was six months ago and draw a line, we cannot scale. The internet will melt down. People wrote more Ph.D. theses about how the internet would die under the load of email and never scale.

Gradually, we started optimizing. We solved the email problem. And when I say "we," I was just watching because I was a 16-year-old who didn't know what the hell was going on. But we as people, as humanity, we solved the problem. We scaled it. The internet failed to scale for Usenet and it succeeded to scale for Usenet so that it could fail to scale for email. Then, it succeeded in scaling for email, so some smartass went and invented MIME, multimedia internet messages, which meant that you could attach things to email. These attachments were 10 times the size of the text because people started sending bigger things, like drawings and pictures and of course, once again, sex.

So, we could scale for email but not for email attachments. Everybody was up in an uproar: "We're never going to be able to scale for email attachments. The internet will surely melt down!" Then we solved it. Until some British guy, Sir Tim Berners Lee (who then was just Tim) invented the web. Now, you could put the pictures into frames.

# The Web Will Destroy the Internet

It was about 1992 when I downloaded and ran the first web browser, NCSA Mosaic, at my university lab. We gathered together three or four friends. We worked for hours to get NCSA Mosaic downloaded and compiled and installed. Then, we launched it and we visited the web. All of it. I can say a sentence not many people can say: In 1992, I visited the entire web in an afternoon. Both sites. Because there were two. I visited both sites, and I thought, *Oh my God. This is going to be huge! The internet will never scale. And just imagine what you could do with sex on the web!* Of course, this became *the* scaling application, as we all know. It has been driving internet development since the beginning, but we don't talk about that in polite company.

> *"I can say a sentence not many people can say: In 1992, I visited the entire web in an afternoon. Both sites. Because there were two. I thought, Oh my god, this is going to be huge! The internet will never scale."*

The internet was failing to scale for the web. People said, "We can never do all of these images and hypertext documents. It will totally fail to scale." And more Ph.D. theses were written and more discussions were had. The internet was still failing to scale. But by now, it had been failing to scale for more than a decade, very gracefully, very successfully.

## VOIP Will Destroy the Internet

Then, someone invented Voice Over IP. Some other people decided, why don't we just replace the entire phone system with the internet? That was a crazy idea. The phone companies then started this massive campaign to inform us of why packet-switched networks could never carry voice. They said, really, the true quality approach to voice was always going to be hierarchical switch networks owned by national monopoly telecom companies because the internet couldn't possibly scale to carry the world's phone calls.

Those same phone companies (the ones still in business) now route all of their phone calls over the internet. First, they didn't want the internet on their phone networks. Then, they allowed the internet on their phone networks. Then, they built their phone networks on top of the internet.

*"First, they didn't want the internet on their phone networks. Then, they allowed the internet on their phone networks. Then, they built their phone networks on top of the internet."*

## Cat Videos Will Destroy the Internet

Then, we started sending videos. And then the internet couldn't scale again because YouTube was going to melt down the internet. Clearly, we needed some content quality and filtering because we can't allow every idiot to go and publish a video about their cat. They said, "There are already a thousand cat videos. If you draw a line from how many cat videos there were yesterday to how many cat videos there are today and if you extrapolate, by the end of this decade, there will be a billion cat videos on the internet!" Which is exactly what happened.

But we scaled. Now, we do 3D video and 4K video.

## Netflix Will Destroy the Internet

When Netflix came along, we saw the same mistake. In 1992, when I visited the first website, my thought was, *Wow, TV is so dead because one day we will be able to transmit movies instantaneously.* If you go and say that to a respectable network researcher in 1992, they call you an idiot. Because, clearly, if we had Netflix in 1992, a single video stream to a single user would melt down the entire internet. Yet, here we are today. By the way, the internet is failing to scale for Netflix and all of the other companies that are doing live video. It will continue to fail to scale incrementally and gracefully. Soon, we'll be doing Oculus Rift holographic 3D, 4K, VR. Then, it will really fail to scale. People will still write Ph.D. theses on why the internet is about to melt down.

# Scaling is a Moving Target

Scaling is a moving target. Scale defines the edge of today's capabilities. As it moves forward, capability increases. The reason for this is really simple: it's because scale is not a goal to achieve; it is a definition of what you can do with the network today. The moment you increase the capacity, the very definition of what you can do with a network today changes because somebody says, "Hang on a second. You mean I can now do $x$, which has 10 times more demand than what

I did before? Let's do some of that." And then, you fail to scale again. Scaling is a moving target. Scale defines the edge of today's capabilities. As it moves forward, capability increases.

> *"Scaling is a moving target. Scale defines the edge of today's capabilities. As it moves forward, capability increases."*

Bitcoin is failing to scale. If we're really lucky, bitcoin will continue to fail to scale gracefully for 25 years, just like the internet.  The very same types of companies that then were saying the internet can never work for all of the email, it can never work to do quality voice calls, it can never work to do quality video, are now making the same kind of corporate arguments about why bitcoin can never do retail payments, it can never do Visa scale, it can never do global scale, and if it's actually adopted, it will collapse. Right now, there are a dozen people writing their Ph.D. theses on how bitcoin will fail, has failed, is dying, was dead, and has died again.

> *"Bitcoin is failing to scale. If we're really lucky, bitcoin will continue to fail to scale gracefully for 25 years, just like the internet."*

There is a beautiful site called bitcoinobituaries.com where you can read the pronouncements of the death of bitcoin since 2009 — regularly, like clockwork every three to six months, major newspapers, scientists, etc., saying, "That's it. Bitcoin is dead." In fact, this has now become an amazing recruitment opportunity because all you have to do is wait for people to hear that bitcoin died, the CEO of Bitcoin was arrested, or bitcoin was shut down by Putin, and then, four months later, someone says, "You know there are some interesting new applications on bitcoin." And they go, "Bitcoin is still there?"

"Bitcoin is still there" is the marketing slogan of this community. If we can just keep doing "bitcoin is still there," people are surprised, they're confounded. It doesn't match their expectations. It's not possible that bitcoin is still there because very serious people with very serious titles, working for very rich companies, told them that bitcoin was not going to be there. But bitcoin is still there, because we are failing to scale gracefully.

# Fee Optimization and Scaling

When we fail to scale during a stress test or a capacity test, when the network is flooded with transactions, what happens? Some users experience a terrible situation. They do a transaction with a 0.1 millibit fee like they've always done, and it takes three days to confirm. During that time, they're freaking out, especially if they're new users. Because new users assume that the money has left their account (there are no accounts in bitcoin) and is en route to the destination account (again, there are no accounts in bitcoin), and therefore is somewhere in limbo in between. The money is really still in their account; it's just that their wallet says it hasn't been confirmed yet. It's either at the source or at the destination, atomically with one transaction. There is no intermediate state. It can't be in limbo because bitcoin doesn't transmit, it settles.

We experience these sudden problems, and some wallets behave intelligently and they increase their fees, sometimes by 100 percent. What this means is instead of it costing 4 cents to send a global transaction in seconds anywhere around the world with full censorship resistance and open innovation and open access to everyone, it takes 8 cents to send that transaction! Clearly, this is an indication, together with the people who waited three days to confirm their transaction, that bitcoin is surely dead now. And some of the developers say, "Oh, I give up. Bitcoin is dead." The newspapers write, "Bitcoin is dead. Transactions are not going through."

Transactions *are* going through. They went through for me. I was running a wallet that was intelligent; it was doing its transaction-fee calculations. What happens in the aftermath of this capacity crunch? We get better wallets.

That's really the essence of a dynamic system responding to pressure because, as we get better wallets, these better wallets calculate fees more correctly. And it's a lot easier to jam the network if there are a lot of dumb wallets doing 0.1 millibit fees, but then, all you have to do is do 0.11 millibit fees and you are king of the hill. Because the other idiots didn't update and jammed the network with their transactions. But if they're able to do 0.12 millibits, now you'll have to do 0.13. Now, we're in a race, and before you know it, you're spending 0.5 millibits, oh dear, on a transaction which of course, if you're a legitimate user, is nothing. If you're trying to jam the network, it starts getting really expensive, really fast.

# Spam Transactions, Legitimate Transactions, Illegitimate Transactions

Which brings up an interesting question: What is a spam transaction? What is a legitimate transaction? What is an illegitimate transaction? There are two ways to answer this. One is a paternalistic, top-down approach that says, this is what is allowed, this is what is not allowed, and by making a list, we will prevent the network from filling to capacity. But that breaks the fundamental capability of bitcoin, which is net neutrality. Bitcoin doesn't care who the sender or the receiver is, what the application is, what the value of the transaction is. All it cares about is, did you pay the fee? If you paid the fee, your transaction is legitimate by definition because you thought it was legitimate enough to attach that fee. The very act of paying the fee legitimizes the transaction. If we start making decisions about what is spam and what is not, we are now choosing the future of bitcoin and constraining it into a set of applications that we can imagine. The brilliant person who creates the application we *can't* imagine—that may look like spam to us—doesn't get carried across the network because we made a top-down decision to say that transaction is illegitimate.

> *"The very act of paying the fee legitimizes the transaction. If we start making decisions about what is spam and what is not, we are now choosing the future of bitcoin and constraining it into a set of applications that we can imagine."*

The other way to do this is to say, how about we use a market to solve this problem. We have a market. We have a currency. Use the market to solve this problem: allow the market to establish the minimum fee that meets the requirements of supply through the miners and their need to propagate blocks fast, and the demand of the users for the applications they care about. If you pay the fee, your transaction is legitimate. There is no spam transaction. There is no such thing as an illegitimate transaction. There are only transactions that did get mined and transactions that didn't have enough fee to get mined.

# Decades of Failing to Scale

This is how bitcoin is going to play out. This is not going to be solved; we will have the scaling discussion every year for decades into the future, hopefully. Every year, we will fail to scale for the next application and succeed to scale for the previous ones. As soon as we do better, people will invent new applications and we will fail to scale again.

*"Every year we will fail to scale for the next application and succeed to scale for the previous ones."*

The internet: failing to scale gracefully for 25 years. Bitcoin: let's keep failing to scale gracefully, and bitcoin is not yet dead.

Thank you.

# A Message from Andreas

## Request for Reviews

Thanks again for reading this book. I hope you enjoyed reading it as much as I enjoyed creating it. If you enjoyed this book, please take a minute to visit the book's page on Amazon or wherever you purchased it and leave a review. This will help the book gain greater visibility in search rankings and reach more people who may be learning about bitcoin for the first time. Your honest feedback also helps me make the next book even better.

## Thank You

I want to take this opportunity to formally thank the community for supporting my work. Many of you share this work with friends, family, and colleagues; you attend events in person, sometimes traveling long distances; and those who are able even support me on the Patreon platform. **Without you I could not do this important work, the work I love, and I am forever grateful.**

Thank you.

# Want More?

## Download a Free Bonus Chapter

If you enjoyed this book and would like to be informed about the next book in the series, get entered into raffles for free copies of books in the series, and keep up with translations and other exciting news, please sign up to The Internet of Money mailing list.

We will not sell or share the list with anyone and will only use it to occasionally send information directly relevant to this book series. As a thank you for signing up, you'll be able to download a FREE bonus chapter that isn't part of any of the other books. The bonus talk is not available for sale, it's available exclusively to mailing list members.

To sign up please scan this:

Or type in this URL:

`theinternetofmoney.info/bonus-chapter-1p`

Or this shorter one:

`bit.ly/2xF7hMa`

# Volume Two Print, Ebook, and Audiobook

This book is the first in a series called *The Internet of Money*. If you enjoyed this book, you might also enjoy Volume Two, which is available in print, ebook, and audiobook formats in the U.S., U.K, Europe, Australia, and elsewhere around the world.

Volume Two contains a "Frequently Asked Questions" section and some of Andreas's most popular talks including:

Introduction to Bitcoin

> Singularity University's IPP Conference; Silicon Valley, California; September 2016;

Blockchain vs Bullshit

> Blockchain Africa Conference at the Focus Rooms; Johannesburg, South Africa; March 2017;

Fake News, Fake Money

> Silicon Valley Bitcoin Meetup at Plug & Play Tech Center; Sunnyvale, California; April 2017;

Immutability and Proof-of-Work, The Planetary-scale Digital Monument

> Silicon Valley Bitcoin Meetup; Sunnyvale, California; September 2016

Currency Wars

> Coinscrum Minicon at Imperial College; London, England; December 2016;

Bubble Boy and the Sewer Rat

> DevCore Workshop at Draper University; San Mateo, California; October 2015;

What is Streaming Money?

> Bitcoin Wednesday Meetup at the Eye Film Museum; Amsterdam, The Netherlands; October 2016;

Rocket Science and Ethereum's Killer App

> Cape Town Ethereum meetup at Deloitte Greenhouse; Cape Town, South Africa; March 2017;

# Keeping Up with Andreas

Find out more about Andreas, including when he is planning to visit your city, on his website at https://www.antonopoulos.com.

You can also follow him on twitter https://www.twitter.com/aantonop or subscribe to his youtube channel at https://www.youtube.com/aantonop.

And of course, Andreas would not be able to do this work without the financial support of the community through Patreon. Learn more about his work and get early access to videos and other exclusive content by becoming a patron at https://www.patreon.com/aantonop.

# Appendix A. Video Links

Each of the chapters included in this book are derived from talks delivered by Andreas M. Antonopoulos at conferences and meetups around the world. Most of the talks were delivered to general audiences, yet some were delivered to limited audiences (like students) for a particular purpose.

Andreas is known for engaging with the audience during his presentations, much of the crowd interaction has necessarily been cut from the text. We encourage you to view the original content, if only to get an idea of what it's like to attend one of these events. All of the videos and many more are available on Andreas's youtube channel — aantonop. https://www.youtube.com/user/aantonop.

Below you'll find a list of the talks we've included in this text, along with locations, dates, and links to the original content.

What Is Bitcoin?

> Disrupt, Start-up, Scale-up Conference; Athens, Greece; November 2013; https://www.youtube.com/watch?v=LA9A1RyXv9s

Peer-to-Peer Money

> Reinvent Money Conference at Erasmus University; Rotterdam, Netherlands; September 2015; https://www.youtube.com/watch?v=n-EpKQ6xIJs

Privacy, Identity, Surveillance and Money

> Barcelona Bitcoin Meetup at FabLab; Barcelona, Spain; March 2016; https://www.youtube.com/watch?v=Vcvl5piGlYg

Innovators, Disruptors, Misfits, and Bitcoin

> Maker Faire at the Henry Ford Museum, Detroit Michigan; July 2014; https://www.youtube.com/watch?v=LeclUjKm408

Dumb Networks, Innovation, and the Festival of the Commons

> O'Reilly Radar Summit at Navy Pier; San Francisco, California; January 2015; https://www.youtube.com/watch?v=x8FCRZ0BUCw

Infrastructure Inversion

> Zurich Bitcoin Meetup; Zurich, Switzerland; March 2016; https://www.youtube.com/watch?v=5ca70mCCf2M

Currency as a Language

> Keynote at the Bitcoin Expo 2014; Toronto, Ontario, Canada; April 2014; https://www.youtube.com/watch?v=jw28y81s7Wo

Bitcoin Design Principles

> Harvard Innovation Lab for an IDEO Workshop; Boston, Massachusetts; June 2015; https://www.youtube.com/watch?v=Ur037LYsb8M

Money as a Content Type

> Bitcoin South Conference; Queenstown, New Zealand; November 2014; https://www.youtube.com/watch?v=6vFgBGdmDgs

Elements of Trust: Unleashing Creativity

> Blockchain Meetup; Berlin, Germany; March 2016; https://www.youtube.com/watch?v=uLpSM3HWU6U

Scaling Bitcoin

> Bitcoin Meetup at Paralelni Polis; Prague, Czech; March 2016; https://www.youtube.com/watch?v=bFOFqNKKns0

# Index

## A

abstract value, 13
access control, 24, 39
account, 107
accounts, 121
adoption, 30, 38, 58, 73, 93
age of, 11
altcoins, 8, 52, 65, 67, 72
   value, 68, 69
an abstraction, 79
animals use of, 11, 78
architecture, 16, 18, 22
as a language, 66
as a liberator, 22
as an application, 71
as emoji, 98
asking permission, 24
ATM, 88
atomic physics, 108
authority, 68, 68
authorization, 97
automobiles, 34, 56, 88

## B

backed by gold, 80
banking, 24, 29, 37, 42, 43, 50, 51, 62, 107, 112
   as a liberator, 22
   inclusion, 3
   neutral network, 25
   the experience, 90
   unbank, 86
barter, 12, 79
bitcoin, 120
breach, 96
byob (be your own bank), 43

## C

cameras, 38

cat videos, 119
censorship, 98
censorship resistant, 27
characteristics of, 13, 78
chemistry, 108
chemistry of, 107
choice, 65
client-server architecture, 17
closed network, 39
comfort noise generation, 61
commons
   festival, 51
   tragedy, 50
communicating value, 12
communication, 12, 22
community, 30, 52, 73
competition, 51, 51, 52, 60
consensus, 2, 2, 47
content, 104
content type, 95
cost of production, 100
creation, 66
creativity, 109
credit cards, 14, 95, 96
crime, 12, 30, 36, 78
criticism, 34
criticisms, 57, 58
crowdfunding, 111
cultural hallucination, 79
currency, 69
   choice, 65
   community, 73
   creation, 66
   evolution, 31
   expression, 66
   index, 72
   paradigm, 65
   sovereignty, 75
   value, 70
   zero-sum game, 66
Currency
   as an application, 71
   meta-politics, 74